Mostly True Confessions

Jean Gonick

Mostly True Confessions

Looking for Love in the Eighties

Random House New York

All rights reserved under International and Pan-American Copyright Conventions. Published in the United States by Random House, Inc., New York, and simultaneously in Canada by Random House of Canada Limited, Toronto.

Portions of this work first appeared in *Detroit News*, the *Hartford Courant*, *The San Francisco Examiner*, *San Francisco Focus* and *New Woman*
Grateful acknowledgment is made to Warner Bros. Music and Mother Bertha Music for permission to reprint lyrics from "Da Doo Ron Ron," by Jeff Barry, Ellie Greenwich and Phil Spector. © 1963 Trio Music Co., Inc./Mother Bertha Music Inc. Used by permission of Warner Bros. Music and Mother Bertha Music. All Rights Reserved.
Grateful acknowledgment for permission to use the title *Mostly True Confessions* is made to *San Francisco Focus*, the city magazine for the Bay Area. Copyright © 1984 by *San Francisco Focus*.

Library of Congress Cataloging-in-Publication Data
Gonick, Jean, 1950–
Mostly True Confessions
1. Single people—United States. I. Title.
HQ800.4.U6G66   1986   305'.90652   85-19364
ISBN 0-394-55131-1

Manufactured in the United States of America
24689753
First Edition

Typography and binding design by J. K. Lambert

*This book is for my parents, Harry and Eleanor,
and my sisters, Cathy and Marsha*

HE:	I say potato.
SHE:	I say potato.
HE:	I say tomato.
SHE:	I say tomato.
HE AND SHE:	Let's call the whole thing off.

Acknowledgments

Special thanks to Cynthia Rubin,
who met me over countless barbecued oysters,
with editor's pencil in hand.

Contents

ALONE

Prologue

"Not only will I never have sex again," I moaned within, while standing alone in my local supermarket, "I'll never again enjoy a meal." This was September 1983, one week after a four-year relationship had blown up in my face. The trip to the supermarket was my first attempt at the feigning of normalcy. It backfired. Suddenly immersed in a perverse nostalgia about the shared food of lovers, I ran home and wrote an essay on the cuisine of a failed romance.

I was not in the habit of doing this. In fact, I'd never done it before.

The day it was published I got a phone call from a man who identified himself as Mel, a forty-five-year-old welder who lived on the peninsula.

"Are you the one who wrote that food thing in today's paper?" he asked.

"Yes, I'm that person," I said. I was still trying to figure out why the newspaper boy hadn't delivered a trumpet fanfare along with my morning edition.

"Well, can I ask you something?" Mel continued. "How did you happen to hit on that 'gentle egg' bit, anyway?"

I had described the preferred breakfast of my ex-boyfriend—scrambled eggs that were not so much scrambled as gently nudged into cooking.

"What do you mean, how did I hit on it?" I was beginning to

get nervous about Mel. Maybe he wasn't Mel at all. Maybe he was my ex, torturing me in a new guise.

"I mean it's uncanny. Shirley and I—Shirley's gone now, you understand, been gone six months—we had a special breakfast called the Fluffy Omelet. See, what you do is you beat the yolks separate from the whites and then fold them together. Makes it real fluffy. We cooked that every weekend. See what I mean by uncanny?"

"Well, Mel, I guess a lot of couples have eggs for breakfast."

"Yeah, guess so. Hey, can I ask you something else? Is your breakup a recent thing or what?"

"Two months." Why was I answering Mel's questions? Why wasn't someone taking me out to brunch in honor of my first publication?

"Gee, it's hard. Believe me, I know how hard it is. But I'm telling you, you just gotta hang in there. You gotta be hopeful." There was the tiniest catch in Mel's gravelly voice. "The thing is, you never know what's waiting around the corner."

No, I thought, you don't. But you can pretty well guess it's not a million dollars or Harrison Ford wanting to buy you a drink.

"Thanks for the encouragement, Mel," I said.

Oddly enough, Mel's call did encourage me. Knowing he and Shirley were forever deprived of their Fluffy Omelet made me feel a modicum less lonely about my own dismal prospect. It also made me more receptive to the urge to write another tale that seized me one evening while my girlfriend was driving me home.

"Thanks for the ride. I have to go look at the wall now," I told her. I walked into my empty apartment, burst into tears, and wrote "Death of a Duck." My ex and I had enjoyed a playful duck lore in our love affair that encompassed ponds, nests, and ruffled feathers. I thought it was unique and I missed it acutely.

The duck story was published in several cities, which is why I received a call from Cleveland. "I'm sixty-three years old," a woman told me, "and my ex-husband and I were bears. Just like you and your ducks. Same thing exactly."

"I guess it's pretty common," I said.

"After he left, I tried to throw out all the bears in the house —the big teddy bears, the little glass bears—but I just couldn't do it."

"It's hard," I agreed.

"What I want to know," she challenged, "is how you could bring yourself to kill that duck the way you did."

I felt strangely accused. "It wasn't exactly premeditated murder. It was more of a spontaneous decision."

The next call was from a local pediatrician. "I didn't know other people experienced this kind of thing," he said. "Frankly, I thought Darlene and I were the only ducks in the world."

"Oh, you were actual ducks?" I asked.

"Our duck life was identical to the one you wrote about. Down to the last quack. And we *have* quacked our last quack."

"I'm sorry."

"I just don't know why it didn't work out between us."

"No one ever does," I said.

"Maybe if I knew exactly why it didn't work out, I could have made it work out," said the pediatrician. He paused. "I know this sounds naïve, but I have to say it again: I thought Darlene and I were the only ducks in the world."

"There must be flocks of them. Or gaggles, or bevies, or whatever it is they congregate in."

Predictably enough, I fell in love a few months later with a man who needed to read the *Pretend You're Sensitive* handbook, (see page 3), and later still with a man who could cook but not quack.

My friends and I meet over lots of comforting pasta and wine and try to figure it out. "If breaking up is so hard to do," a friend asked me, inspired by Neil Sedaka's golden oldie emanating from my radio, "then why is everybody always doing it?"

I served her more linguini. "Maybe romantic love isn't the most important thing in the world," I suggested. "Maybe we should look for the higher ideal."

"Like love of community? A spiritual life?"

"Why not?"

The song ended and my friend drained her wineglass happily. She looked at me and said something that cheered me even more than the linguini did. "Take Mother Teresa. Do you think she worries about a Saturday night date?"

Somehow I don't think she does. I'm just trying to figure out if that's a helpful thing to know.

Looking

1. Sensitivity

It was clear to me the first time I went out with Greg that he'd never read—indeed, never even heard of—the *Pretend You're Sensitive* handbook. After a five-hour conversation he was still ignorant of my surname, line of work, or chronological position among my siblings. I, on the other hand, was intimately acquainted with the rather tedious details of his divorce, the status of his investments, and his abhorrence of beets, two slices of which he deposited onto my salad. Did I, too, hate beets? Greg never asked.

Greg thought a cognac at my house would cap the evening well; I convinced him at my front door that it would not. I was astonished when he suggested we go out again; it seemed to me he could go out with a coffee table and have the same experience. I didn't think I could take another night of dispassionate soliloquy, so I offered to make a deal.

"I'll see you after you read the first five chapters of the *Pretend You're Sensitive* handbook."

"I've never heard of it."

"I know. It was written for men. Men like yourself. You'll find it in the men's studies section of your neighborhood bookstore. In paperback."

"There's no such thing as a men's studies section, is there?"

"Sure. It's all those sections that aren't women's studies."

A week later Greg came over, assuring me that he'd done his homework. And indeed he had; I could tell immediately, because he used my first name three times before he even sat down. Rule number one in the *Pretend You're Sensitive* handbook: "Pretend you can differentiate your date from other women."

"Greg, hello, Greg, it's good to see you again, Greg, please sit down, Greg," I responded eagerly. I wanted Greg to know that I knew that he knew that I wasn't a coffee table. "What's in the bag?" I asked while he seated himself across the room from me, sensitive to my possible need for space.

He extracted a bottle of what looked like good wine. At least, I'd never seen it advertised on television. "A sensitive choice," I said. I waited to see if he'd lecture me on the history of the winery that produced it or give me a forty minute update on his own extensive wine cellar, as he had the week before. He did neither. "*Very* sensitive," I repeated, uncorking the wine.

Greg was doing so well that I rewarded him by asking how his law practice was going. He cleared his throat and was two minutes into a moment-by-moment technical narration of his work week when he abruptly stopped mid-sentence. I could almost see rule number two of the *Pretend You're Sensitive* handbook flashing before his eyes.

"Enough about law," he laughed. "Where do *you* work?"

"Over there," I said, indicating a desk on the other side of the room.

"Oh," he said, tossing back his wine. "Self-employed, huh?" I nodded and waited to see if he'd ask what I *did* at the desk, but he only requested more wine, using my first name twice while doing so. I told myself he was only a beginner, that five chapters could not remake the man.

We drove to my favorite Thai restaurant after I assured Greg that I'd never yet encountered a beet in Thai cuisine. We sat down, unfolded our napkins, and looked at our chopsticks. Greg signaled for the waiter, opened his mouth to speak, then closed it.

"A fork?" I prompted.

"Nah. I'll give these a try," he said rubbing the chopsticks together as if trying to ignite the light of cultural exchange.

"Do you like squid?" I asked, perusing the menu. Rule number three: "Pretend to be open to new experiences, beginning with the gastronomical."

"Each and every tentacle," he lied.

The next time I saw Greg he'd read five more chapters of the *Pretend You're Sensitive* handbook and was able to ask me if I had an immediate family. Rule number four: "Notice she has parents, perhaps siblings. Ask about them." Midway through dinner I realized that he had studied the chapter on eye contact thoroughly; he could synchronize looking me in the eye and using my first name perfectly. The effect was devastating; I almost had to leave the table. Greg was pretending to be so sensitive that I almost thought he was.

"What kind of work do you do at your desk?" he asked me, maintaining that electric visual connection while sliding the beets off his salad plate.

What a sensitive question! "I write."

"Terrific."

I smiled.

"Really terrific," he said, ripping into his steak.

I stopped smiling. "I lied," I lied. "I don't write. I give manicures out of my home."

"Yeah?" he asked, mid-chew. "Well, that's terrific, too."

I told Greg I wouldn't see him again until he completed the *Pretend You're Sensitive* handbook and reread the prologue outlining the philosophy of pretensions to sensitivity. He promised to do so and called me two days later.

"I get it. I was supposed to ask you what *kind* of writing you do." I knew every legal case he'd ever worked on.

"Right," I said. "The idea is to feign curiosity even though you don't feel it."

"Right," he said, hanging up. He called back immediately. "Sorry," he said. "What kind of writing do you do?"

I sighed. "Greg, I appreciate your efforts, eating squid tentacles and everything, but I just don't think this is going to work out."

"I live for challenges," he protested. "Let me attack this like a law book. I wasn't editor of *Law Review* for nothing, you know. I'll see you in two weeks and by then I promise I'll be the most sensitive man in the western hemisphere."

I was too curious to refuse. I sensed that Greg really was the kind of man who could master anything once he set his mind to it. Unfortunately, when he called me again I had my period and didn't want to see him or anyone else. I was bloated and homicidal.

"How are you?" he asked.

"Not well." I was not about to report the source of my anguish to a man who'd told me his ex-wife's menstrual cramps were all in her head.

"I'm really sorry to hear that," he said, actually sounding sorry. I looked at the receiver askance. "Is there anything I can do?"

What the hell, I thought. "I'm just cranky because I have my period."

"I have just the cure for you," he said. A shrink? A head bandage? "May I come over and practice medicine without a license?"

Greg was now so sensitized, he'd even become playful. "Sure," I said, intrigued.

Fifteen minutes later Greg was handing me a glass of Spanish sherry and two aspirin. He had obviously mastered the handbook. I was beginning to like him very much, despite my homicidal condition.

"Here's to the end of misogyny in the medical profession." He toasted me with his own glass of sherry. "May they seek and find a cure for cramps." He dispensed two aspirin for himself.

"Headache?" I asked.

"No, sympathetic cramps."

I almost choked on my sherry. Oh no, I thought. Had Greg crossed that subtle line from sensitive male to hypersensitive male? I had heard of such cases.

"You probably need a good meal," he offered.

"I do have a hormonal yen for a cheeseburger," I admitted. We walked down the street to a franchise restaurant and ordered burgers and shakes. When they arrived, Greg handed his silver-ware to the waitress and asked for chopsticks.

"Ketchup?" she asked, confused.

"No, *chopsticks.*"

"Greg, you can't eat a cheeseburger with chopsticks," I said gently. "It's very sensitive of you to try, though."

Tears welled up in his eyes.

"I'm sorry, Greg. I didn't mean to hurt your feelings."

He dabbed his eye with his napkin.

"Hey, is he okay?" the waitress asked me.

"Sure. He's just, you know, hypersensitive," I explained, cutting Greg's cheeseburger in half for him. "Please, Greg, cheer up. You can have my fries."

He brightened and started to eat. "After this," he said, "let's go back to your place and read aloud to each other. I've got *Pride and Prejudice* in my car."

"Austen? I thought you only read Norman Mailer."

"Oh, no. Give me a nineteenth-century English novel any time. The only twentieth-century literature I'm interested in is yours."

"What?" I almost blinded myself with my straw.

"You know, your writing. I'd like to read everything you've ever written, if I may. Since childhood."

This was too much. Greg had paid more attention to me in the past hour than he had during the whole span of our acquaintance. It was making me sort of dizzy.

"Greg, you don't have to read everything I've written. Just one story would make me happy. And you don't have to read Jane Austen, although she is wonderful and would probably change your life."

"I don't?" He tried not to look relieved, but it didn't quite work.

"Maybe John Cheever." Why waste this new literary zeal?

"Okay," he conceded. "Let's go to your place and read chapters of *The Wapshot Chronicle* to each other."

"Fine. Let's go."

"In a minute. I'm still hungry." He called the waitress back and, while I sat in a bloated daze, asked for a side order of beets from the salad bar.

Greg looked kind of cute with his lips stained with beet juice. My cramps were starting to subside.

"Do you love me?" he asked.

"I don't know," I answered. "Let's go read and see."

2. Fashion Victims

I studied the art of dressing under the tutelage of Ms. Leslie Harris, a friend and co-worker whose clothes are always perfect. My education was inaugurated in a state of coercion, and it happened one night when Leslie watched me select my outfit for an office party.

"What are you going to wear?" she asked me, as we stood in my bedroom. My eyes roamed the room and settled on their first identifiable target: a red sweater still encased in dry-cleaner plastic. There was half the outfit. "That," I pointed. My glance then traveled three more feet to an armchair over which were draped still clean, nearly unwrinkled black pants. "And that," I concluded.

"That's how you choose your clothes?"

"Sure. Proximity and cleanliness."

Leslie sighed heavily.

"Look, what I really want to wear is my bathrobe," I said.

Leslie sighed again. My fashion oblivion had infuriated her for years but this bathrobe remark was the final, intolerable offense. "You have to let me take you shopping," she pleaded.

"I hate to shop." I truly did. Stores frightened me; I was dazed by the plethora of merchandise, almost paralyzed with indecision.

"Bite your tongue. Let's just say your shopping potential is still untapped." Leslie prefers shopping to all other worldly activities, and comes from a family of women who borrow each other's earrings and can discuss hemlines for hours at a time. "Come see what I bought," is the family mantra. To visit them is to drop in on the barbecue at Twelve Oaks in *Gone with the Wind:* women being women, engaged in talk of chemises and rose water. I have always found it charming and incomprehensible.

"I don't want to learn to shop," I whined. "I don't approve of women spending their hard-earned money on clothes competition. I refuse to be a fashion victim."

"I'm proud to be one," Leslie breathed.

I resisted further. "Men don't notice what women wear, so why bother?" A man had once told me that he liked a nice ass and a sweet smile on a woman, and that was about all he saw. I had decided to base most of my fashion views on this one remark.

"Some men *do* notice, but that's not the point anyway. We don't dress for men—we dress for ourselves. Nice clothes make you confident."

"I'm already confident."

"No, you only think you're confident," she said, slyly.

Leslie was right; my confidence was plummeting with every word she spoke.

"Now go ahead and get dressed," she directed, "and tomorrow morning I'm taking you downtown."

Her insidious seed was already firmly planted. "Get dressed?" I shrieked. "But I haven't got a thing to wear!"

When Leslie met me in front of Macy's the next morning, I was in jeans and a devastated blouse and she was, as usual, flawlessly coordinated.

"You look terrific even when you shop," I sighed, already feeling defeated.

"You never know who you'll run into," she explained.

"Oh yes, I do. No one. No one is exactly who I always run in-to."

"Don't forget the sales people. We want them to know who they're dealing with."

"Right, Christie Brinkley and Bozo the Clown. Is this going to cost me a fortune?" My unfashionable heels were instinctively digging themselves into the sidewalk.

"We're not making any actual purchases today," she informed me. "This is a preliminary field trip. I want to get you used to the visuals."

We entered the store and Leslie turned to me solemnly. "The first rule," she intoned, "is to stay away from the junior depart-ment. One should never shop to the beat of bad music." I nodded. "The second rule is to shop early in the morning, before the crowds come in."

"It's nine-thirty," I observed. "It couldn't be any earlier."

"And the third rule is to not shop when you're depressed."

"Too late," I said, feeling that familiar department-store ma-laise envelop me.

I stood in my traditional paralytic stance while Leslie dug effi-ciently through the racks. "This would be nice on you," she said, holding up a teal-blue drop-waisted dress. Of course, I didn't know the blue was teal until Leslie told me.

"Mona told me I shouldn't wear drop waists. She said my hips were too big."

Leslie frowned. "Did you ever notice that Mona was born without an ass? And that she doesn't like you very much?"

"Oh?"

"Rule number four: Don't listen to people who don't have your best interests at heart. Listen to *me*—I actually want you to look nice."

Leslie began taking on the contours of Annie Sullivan, the only true teacher who would lead me out of fashion darkness and silence. "Shall I try on the dress?" I asked, now the docile student.

"No. We must proceed slowly. Today we merely look." She continued to hold up unexpected items, fearlessly separating the teal-blue wheat from the unexciting chaff, soliciting my opinion and horrified to see that I never had one.

"It's not that you have bad taste," she said, after two hours. "It's that you haven't got any. You're a fashion virgin."

"I'm hungry," I complained. "Let's have lunch."

"Fine, this is enough for the first day." She ushered me outside and stopped at a newsstand. "Give me ten bucks," she ordered. I complied; she gave me an armful of fashion magazines. "This is your first reading assignment. Have it done by Tuesday."

"What about lunch?"

"You can't afford it now."

Obediently, I went through each magazine page by page, trying to absorb the concept of fashion. Leslie was right: the models, whose foremothers had undoubtedly all attended the Twelve Oaks barbecue, beamed with the confidence of being well dressed. They also beamed with the confidence of being twenty-one, gorgeous and incredibly well paid.

"You've completed your prerequisite of visual exposure," Leslie told me Tuesday as we entered Sak's. "Today we use a dressing room."

I stripped to my unfashionable underclothes and stood mutely as Leslie brought in skirt after blouse after dress.

"Why are all the shoulders padded?" I asked, naïvely.

"Norma Kamali," she replied. I thought it was some sort of incantation. "Nor-ma-ka-mah-lee?" I repeated.

"Try this on," she suggested, handing me a hot-pink jacket. It was surprisingly wonderful.

"A jacket can virtually transform a wardrobe," she instructed. "Push the sleeves up a bit. Now turn up the collar. Put your hands in your pockets, toss your hair, and look pissed off. There. Perfect. You're a model."

"I think I like it," I said, hesitantly. I sort of expected Leslie to join me in a chorus of "The Rain in Spain Stays Mainly in the Plain."

"If you like it, then describe it," she challenged.

I stared at my hot-pink reflection and remembered the magazines. "It's the Wow-Pow-Now Look."

"Exactly. Congratulations."

"Why does it cost eighty dollars?"

"Don't ruin the moment. Next week you'll be ready to pick something all by yourself."

My education continued. Leslie conducted lecture-demonstrations on fabric by having me compare the feel of two different blouses. I stroked them and pretended I understood the difference. She explained how to buy shoes that would never hurt. I didn't tell her that my remedy for painful shoes was to wear Spanish Inquisition earrings and an itchy wool sweater, thereby making myself so totally uncomfortable that I could no longer isolate the pain in my feet. She taught me about control-top pantyhose and didn't flinch when I asked her if they also came in out-of-control.

"You're making remarkable progress," she said proudly. "I think you'll be ready for your diploma as soon as you select something to wear to Jeff's barbecue."

A barbecue? Had the Twelve Oaks plantation been relocated to Jeff's Pacific Heights home? Would I, like Scarlett, be torn between my green sprigged muslin dress and my black bombazine? Would Mammy lace me into my corset? Was I up to this?

"This is the aspect of fashion that I hate," I reminded her. "I hate the illusion that I'll have a better time at a party if I'm well dressed."

"But you will."

"No, I won't. I only have fun at a party if there's someone to flirt with. And you know Jeff's friends as well as I do: complacent couples, a few unhappy women, and the Peter Pan contingency."

"He's barbecuing oysters," Leslie said to entice me.

"Okay. I don't need to flirt."

I was all decked out in well-cut white linen when Leslie came to pick me up for the party. My earrings were compelling, my shoes attractive and painless. Leslie was, in a word, amazed. Was it only yesterday that I learned to differentiate turtleneck from cowl, and to identify cowl as preferable?

"I like this," she said, feeling my sleeve. "What did it cost?"

"It was on sale. I got it for less than fifty."

She nodded approvingly. "Quick! Are Anne Klein and Calvin Klein related?"

"No!" I shouted triumphantly.

"And who should wear miniskirts?"

"Nobody!"

Jeff's party looked like every other party I'd been to in the last six months: fabulous food and a dearth of sexual tension. I handed Jeff a bottle of champagne, greeted his girlfriend, and stationed myself near the outdoor grill. A man shucking oysters smiled at me and said hello.

"Hello," I answered. "Are you married?"

"Yes," he replied.

"Nice not to meet you," I said, turning away. I never used to ask this intrusive question, but I got tired of unwittingly dating men who forgot to mention their marital status. A direct question saves a lot of time.

"Having fun?" Leslie asked me. She was wearing, as usual, $400 worth of clothes. She looked wonderful. But so, finally, did I.

"Oh yeah, this is a real hoot," I said.

"But don't you feel confident? You look great in white."

"I love my white linen dress. But that doesn't make that handsome oyster shucker any more available."

She looked over at the married man by the grill. "Don't despair. Jeff's turning on the music. People will dance. You'll be a white-linen vision."

"This is 1985 in San Francisco. The men will dance with each other." Indeed, they were already beginning to.

"Look," Leslie hissed. "I said nice clothes would make you feel more confident—I didn't say they would change the social structure of contemporary urban life! If you're going to be ignored at a party, wouldn't you rather look your best while it's happening?"

"No, actually. It sort of makes it worse."

"Not for me. The more miserable I feel, the better I need to look."

I was beginning to hate Leslie, Christie Brinkley, and the whole fashion industry. What the hell, I thought. I didn't care how I looked or who talked to me—I was going to drink champagne and eat as many oysters as Jeff would allow. And I'd dance with myself if I had to. I returned to the grill and began loading oysters onto a plastic plate.

"You didn't let me finish," said the oyster shucker, as he handed me a lemon wedge. "I'm married, but I've been separated from my wife for a year. She moved in with our tax man."

"Oh," I said, unimpressed.

"I've been at this grill for an hour. Would you mind if I took a break and sampled the fruits of my labor with you?"

"Do what you want," I said, mentally pushing up my sleeves, tossing my hair, and trying to look like a true fashion bitch.

He sat beside me and poured out two glasses of champagne. I ate silently, staring icily into the distance.

"I'm a pushover for white linen," he said.

I dropped an oyster on the lawn. "You are?" I asked, suddenly grinning ear to well-dressed ear.

"You're the best-dressed woman here."

"I am?"

Life is a wonderful thing. My oyster shucker proceeded to confide in me the story of his failed marriage, his career plans, and his need for my phone number. I gave him my card and immediately started agonizing over what to wear when I next saw him.

"Excuse me a moment," I said, speeding across the patio to Leslie's side.

"I need more clothes," I squealed to her. "Can you come shopping with me tomorrow?"

"You're a clothes graduate now," she insisted. "You don't need me any more."

Could Leslie be right? Was I now qualified to waste days of my life obsessing about every article of clothing I wore? Could I now, without supervision, spend half my paycheck on vain pursuits?

Leslie recognized the glint in my eye. "I never thought I'd see the day. You're a real live fashion victim."

"An expert teacher once told me she was proud to be one."

"And aren't you proud?"

I looked at my oyster shucker who waited for me patiently. I didn't care what he wore; he happened to look beautiful in jeans and a T-shirt. Would he really like me less in similar attire?

"He loves this dress, Leslie. Do you think he'll still love it if he sees me in it twice?"

"No, he'll think you're lame. You'd better go downtown tomorrow and get something new."

"All right," I promised, still the diligent student. I returned to the shucker and spent the rest of the afternoon with him, sharing champagne and life stories. I guess we shared a little too much champagne because, much as he admired my dress, he couldn't help spilling neon orange barbecue sauce down the front of it.

"I'm sorry!" he said. "I'll pay to have it cleaned!"

"Don't worry, clothes are meaningless," I assured him.

3. But Are You Married?

Robert patted his own balding head, as if for reassurance, before entering the smoky, cavernous room. It was his first Literary Alliance party, and he'd come alone, leaving Margaret, his distinctly unliterary wife, at home. His head was wet; it was raining outside. He already missed Margaret, which surprised him. They had agreed to make their marriage a "spacious" one, where they could each pursue their own interests, incurring neither guilt nor wrath. But so far in their six-month-old union, the issues of space and freedom had been purely theoretical: they had been together constantly. And now, on his first evening of autonomy, Robert missed her. He forged ahead to the bar, looking for familiar faces.

No one looked familiar, but at least there was free imported beer. He opened one and drank it amidst dyads and triads of chatty writers. As always, he surveyed the crowd quickly to see how many men under thirty were already losing their hair. It was difficult to assess age in this dimly lit room, but there seemed to be at least five. Good. He looked at the women and, save for one or two, Margaret was better looking than any of them. If he could not have his beautiful wife on his arm in public, it was comforting to know she was waiting for him in their new condominium.

Robert could not stop from smiling. Marriage was wonderful.

Behind him, two women discussed salads with great animation.

"It's the first thing I take away points for," said one. "If they say it's a tossed green salad, then they should toss it before serving it, for God's sake. The dressing has to be evenly distributed. There's nothing worse than a puddle of dressing sitting on top of a green salad."

"You're right," agreed the other one. "How do you feel about unpeeled cucumber slices?"

"Another sign of kitchen laziness. It's rampant." Robert recognized this woman as Heidi Sims, a food writer for the Sunday paper he read. She was good; he could still recall lines from her recent treatise on eggplant. He turned to see what she looked like. She was blonde, pretty, on a par with Margaret.

"Do you think goat cheese has run its course?" he asked Heidi directly. Before he married Margaret, he had mastered the party art of conversational interjection. It still worked. Her friend chuckled and turned to greet someone else. Heidi returned his grin.

"Only in my column," she laughed, "but not in reality. I don't think great food can *ever* run its course."

He remembered making a goat cheese omelet for Margaret after reading Heidi's goat cheese article. Margaret hadn't liked it. "Food writing is fun, at least the way you do it," he said. "I'm just a dull travel writer. I deal with regional cuisine sometimes, but not with much authority." He'd probably overcooked the omelet, he decided.

"There's nothing dull about travel," Heidi assured him with what Robert felt showed a generous spirit. "In fact, I'd like to get into travel writing. Tell me how you did it."

"Let me get another beer first. Can I get you one? They're good. Or at least they're imported."

"Sure, I'll take one, thanks. The wine's dreck."

When Robert returned with the beer, Heidi was declining a

dance with a tall guy with a lot of hair. "I'm networking," she explained. "Maybe later."

Robert felt a funny twinge. "Want to dance?" he asked. "I mean, we can dance and then talk. Or we can talk while we dance." He wasn't sure he was networking; it felt more like flirting. He thought they were similar.

"Okay," she said. They took their beers with them and danced to old James Brown hits. It was too loud to talk, but not too loud for Heidi to yell, "God, I love this song!" when James sang "I Wake Up in a Cold Sweat." Robert hated James Brown, but he liked the way Heidi danced.

The tall guy with too much hair tapped Heidi on the shoulder between dances. Robert turned aside and swigged beer while she answered the tall guy's question. "Robert, let's go discuss travel," she said, just as James started to sing "This Is a Man's World." Much as he disliked James, he knew he'd like to dance a slow one with Heidi. He took her in his arms; she complied.

It wasn't that Margaret wouldn't have come to the party if he'd wanted her to; she was very supportive about public accompaniment in marriage. And even though she wasn't particularly literary (she was a quantitative type, studying to become a CPA), she was sweet natured and could usually have a good time anywhere. But they had agreed to give each other room to breathe, and the semiannual Literary Alliance party provided the perfect opportunity to test his lungs. He wondered briefly if room to breathe also meant room to dance.

"Do you like to go out dancing?" Heidi asked against his shoulder.

"Not much any more," he admitted. Not since marriage, he meant.

"I don't do it enough either," she said. "It's good to remember how fun it can be. Works off all those fattening meals, too."

"You don't have to worry about that," he said, hugging her slightly.

She looked up at him, blue eyes opened wide. "Do you know how many calories there are in an ounce of goat cheese?" she asked in mock horror.

"No, how many?"

She laughed. "It's so good, who cares?" He hugged her again. He hugged her until the end of the record when she said, "So. Travel. Tell me how to get into it. I'd love to take some of those free trips." She listened attentively while he recited his professional transition story: a double major in business and journalism, a growing disaffection for the business world and a lucky publication of his first travel piece in a national magazine. He'd been almost instantly launched into freelance success. Not only could he support himself, but he'd also been to twenty-seven different countries to date.

"Amazing," said Heidi. "Are the writers ever allowed to bring a guest for free? Especially if the guest can take photographs?" She smiled charmingly. He wondered if she minded balding men. Women always said they didn't care about those things, but it was hard to believe.

"You can always take someone on a cruise. They don't expect anyone to be alone on a ship."

"Real *Love Boat*, right?"

"You might say that." He thought of a Caribbean cruise with Heidi. He'd wear a hat to protect his balding head, and she would tan to a burnished perfection and her hair would lighten more in the sun. He stroked her yellow hair without thinking, then withdrew. He didn't want to kiss her, he decided. He wanted to know that she wanted him to.

"So who do you take on these cruises?"

"Margaret. My wife."

Robert was astonished to see Heidi's eyes narrow by half. "You're married?"

"Yes."

"Is your wife here?"

"No, I came alone."

"Why?"

He felt distinctly cross-examined. "She's not a writer; she doesn't care about these functions. We do things separately sometimes." Well, one time anyway. "She doesn't mind that I'm here."

"No, of course she doesn't mind. But I think I do."

Robert realized the Caribbean fantasy had been brutally interrupted. "What do you mean?"

"I mean that you've just wasted an hour of my time."

"Wasted? Weren't we having a pleasant conversation?" He was beginning to take offense.

"I know plenty of people I can have pleasant conversations with. And so do you. I didn't come here for that."

"No, you came to network, and so did I. And we networked, right?"

The only thing Heidi hated more than Velveeta cheese was the word "network," even though she occasionally used it, and then only because she knew it would be understood. "Do you honestly believe I drove forty minutes through the rain to drink beer and make business connections?"

"Of course. That's what 'Literary Alliance' is all about."

"Not for me it isn't. I joined it to meet men."

"That can't be the only reason."

"It's the main one."

"Well, that's candid."

"More candid than you've been," she chastised. Her arms were folded across her chest, her beer forgotten on the floor. "Why didn't you tell me right away that you were married?"

Robert thought before answering. "Because I was afraid you wouldn't talk to me for very long if you knew."

"So you withheld the information."

"I wouldn't call it *withholding.*"

"Postponement? Until directly asked?"

"Yeah, maybe."

"That's misrepresentation, isn't it?"

"What is this—a court of law?" Robert was incredulous. "Listen, I'm not defined solely by my marriage. It's not the first fact I have to reveal about myself."

"It is if you're flirting."

"So who's flirting? I'm networking!"

Heidi unfolded her arms, held them out in frustration. "How can you be so sure of the difference? I'm not sure myself half the time."

Robert heard the echo of his own confusion and wanted to sound clearheaded.

"Flirtation is sexual, and networking is purely business," he offered. "I guess."

"Exactly—you guess. It shouldn't be guesswork, though. I think it's too important."

Robert was feeling progressively worse. "You know, I should tell you—I love my wife. We have a terrific marriage and I've never been unfaithful to her." He knew this was hardly impressive after six months of wedded bliss. "And I don't intend to be," he added.

"If I were married," Heidi said wistfully, "I'd be home with my husband, and we'd be lying on the couch reading novels together."

"Margaret's not a reader."

"Then if I were you, I'd be home watching TV and drinking brandy with her."

"You can't do that every night."

"I think I could."

"You might find it boring."

Heidi shook her head. "I wouldn't." She paused. "You know why you're really lucky?" she asked. It was Robert's turn to shake his head. "You get to make love to someone you actually know and like and who won't give you a fatal disease."

Something about her insinuation into their sexual life made

him stand up very tall. "I probably *will* make love to her when I go home," he said, instantly regretting the inanity of it. Still, she had set him off.

"Good for you. Maybe you should go home now and do just that. Home is where married people should be. Home is what marriage is all about."

"That's ridiculous. Married people need their space."

The only word Heidi hated more than "network" was "space" unless it referred to the outer one. "I don't see why. I've got so much space I could choke on it. If I got married, it'd be to fill up the space, so I could stay home on a rainy night and skip noisy, stupid parties like this one."

"Hey, this is a great party."

"Well, it's a nice diversion for you. You come alone, make some business contacts and a few idle flirtations, then go home to a loving wife. And I go home and turn my electric blanket up to 900."

"That's not my fault."

The tall guy with too much hair passed by them, leading an exotic brunette by the hand. Heidi winced.

"So when in a conversation do you think someone should say they're married?" he asked.

"What's wrong with immediately? What's wrong with 'Hello, I'm Robert and I'm married'?"

"You're kidding."

"I'm not."

Robert was beginning to feel sorry for her until he saw her blue gaze settling on his bald spot. He glowered at her for a moment, unsure what to say next.

"Good night," she said, turning on her heel and solving the problem for him.

What a pathetic, pretty, and not altogether unpleasant woman, he thought, his head burning despite the absence of Caribbean sun. He was sorry he'd ruined her evening. He'd only meant to have some fun, but having fun was astonishingly difficult and autonomy hard to negotiate. He felt strangely drained and wanted to go home to Margaret, lovely Margaret who could cook at least as well as Heidi Sims, with her overrated eggplant and fattening goat cheese. Margaret was wonderful. He would drink just one more beer and then drive home and tell her so.

4. New Math

I've just been introduced to the New Math, which is horrific for me because math courses are the ones I always failed in school. I can't quite figure out these new equations.

A forty-four-year-old doctor facilitated my introduction by telling me at a party that he only dated women in their mid- to late twenties.

"Let me get this straight," I said, balancing a drink and a hefty serving of pâté. "I'm a decade younger than you are, but hypothetically I'm already too old for you. Right?"

"There's nothing hypothetical about it." He grinned, pâté glistening on his tie. "You *are* too old for me."

I looked intently at the sourdough and pâté I held in one hand and wondered briefly if this doctor would like me better if it were suddenly transformed into a Twinkie. Something innocent, festively juvenile.

Granted, this man's favorite book was *Jonathan Livingston Seagull,* so his criteria for anything might be hastily dismissed. Still, I was curious and started reading personal ads to see for myself. After two hours of study I knew three things:

1. Men want women who are young and slim.
2. Women want men who are solvent and not mean.

3. Everyone wants to take long walks in front of the fireplace. The male penchant for the young and slim dominated almost every ad I read, trivializing all other attributes. Would a man want a schizophrenic neo-Nazi if said Nazi were young and slim enough? I suspected that he might.

I'm not stupid; I understand the appeal of the young. Last year I dated a twenty-five-year-old and he was extremely cute. He had zest for life, tight skin, and was refreshingly unembittered. But the liaison didn't last long and we almost never went out in public. Arthur and I recently talked over the phenomenon of the Younger Date. A longtime friend of my family, Arthur is fifty, divorced, and egalitarian enough to date women of all ages.

"I date women twenty years younger than myself when I'm depressed," he admitted to me. Arthur is Republican, but honest.

"Because they're energetic and hopeful and they lift your spirits?"

"No, because they think I'm brilliant."

"Oh, yeah." I thought back to my twenty-five-year-old. Everything I said amazed him. "Gee, I never thought about it like that before," had been his standard response. Of course—he hadn't had time to think about anything yet; he'd only been out of college for twenty seconds. Initially I had basked in his adoration of my intellect, but this was soon followed by ennui and then nausea. It was sickening to impress someone that easily. It was even worse to be impressed with myself for being able to do so.

"But, Arthur, doesn't that get tedious before too long?"

"Depends on how depressed I am. I can date a twenty-year-old for a good six months if I'm faintly suicidal. She'll think I'm Adlai Stevenson, William Butler Yeats, and Linus Pauling all rolled into one. Not that she'll know who any of those men are. But it does wonders for my self-esteem."

"You're disgusting," I said, with a laugh. One cannot offend Arthur. I've tried.

He narrowed his eyes at me. "I can get away with it."

If Arthur is pathetic, he at least does not attribute nonexistent qualities to his youthful love objects. My cousin's ex-husband has been on the Projection Merry-Go-Round every day of the five years following their divorce. I like Dennis. He takes me to lunch every time he falls in love. The younger the woman, the deeper his euphoria, and the better the restaurant.

"This is it," he announces every time. "This woman has wisdom beyond her years. Just incredible. Ours will be a union of ecstasy, not of bondage."

"How many years does she have wisdom beyond?"

"Twenty-three, but that's not the point. She has a very old soul."

"She's a Hindu?"

"She's a goddess."

Dennis was insane enough to introduce me to the goddess a week later; she was bright and sweet and she asked me where I bought my gray linen jacket. After three more weeks Dennis fell out of love, assuming, I guess, that goddesses don't bruise.

The New Math intrigues me: if a twenty-year age difference is good, is a thirty-year difference better, and the gap of forty years better yet? Can a woman, in fact, ever be too young?

My friend Edward just turned forty; his wife is eight years his junior. One afternoon he and I were drinking tea in a downtown hotel that drew an extremely senior crowd. He studied the faces around him, fascinated, it seemed, by a condition he thought might somehow elude him.

"Women age more noticeably than men do," he observed.

I looked at the gray heads around me, poured cream into my cup. "No, they don't," I said.

"They do," he insisted.

I looked again and saw no difference in the signs of age between one gender and the other. A wrinkle is a wrinkle is a wrinkle.

"It annoys you when women aren't pretty, doesn't it?" I said.

Edward's wife is a petite Spanish beauty. "I prefer the company of pretty women," he admitted.

"Women don't age just to irritate you, you know," I reminded him. "Everyone ages, even you."

"I won't age like *that,*" he vowed, pushing away the scones and butter. "I'll take care of myself."

"Age any way you like," I said, pushing the scones back in his direction. "You won't be penalized for it." I dumped half a pitcher of fattening, aging cream into his teacup. "God help your wife when she turns forty," I said.

"Lucinda will always be beautiful."

"I hope she leaves you for a twenty-two-year-old rock star," I said.

Edward was not amused. I guess he hasn't reached that advanced level yet in his New Math skills.

5. Thwarted Matchmaker

I'd enjoyed almost a year of uninterrupted domestic serenity
with Joseph when I felt a major matchmaking impulse coming
on. The urge is fairly predictable; as soon as I become comfort-
able with my own mated bliss, I inevitably decide everyone I know
should be just as lucky as I am. I've noticed that not everyone
shares this perhaps misguided impulse, this need to orchestrate a
setup. I, however, have always entertained the illusion that I can
manipulate the universe.

My best friend, Charlene, had been looking for love for two
years. Making that dangerous transition from desperate to resigned, she was spending her Friday nights eating pot roast with
Joseph and me rather than going out in pursuit of romance.

"I like being with you and Joseph," she insisted. "You're like
family."

"And we love having you," I assured her. "But I think you need
a romance."

"Too much investment for too little returns. I've already had
romance. That part of my life is over."

Charlene didn't say that to be melodramatic. She believed, at
age thirty, that it was true.

"Remember sex?" I said.

"Frankly, no."

"Come on, Joseph," I urged. "Don't you know anyone at school?" Joseph teaches high-school English.

"Charlene's too good for the guys I know," he said. Men always say that when you're trying to implement a matchmaking plan. I can't tell if they mean it (Joseph's fellow teachers *are* pretty resistible) or if they're trying to protect their friends. It's a biological thing; men just don't possess the matchmaking chromosome. I don't understand it: I know men get just as lonely as women do. Joseph told me so. "Besides," he added, "teachers don't make any money. As you know."

"You don't care about men having money, do you?" I asked Charlene.

"I'm used to poverty," she said with a shrug. Charlene is a social worker, and the only person I know who earns less than Joseph. It always horrifies me that while she finds jobs for refugees, and Joseph passes the light of knowledge on to the young, I make twice what they do because I happen to work in advertising.

"You shouldn't assume Charlene's lonely," Joseph admonished me.

"You shouldn't refer to me as if I weren't here," Charlene said.

"We're family," I said. "We can be rude. Are you lonely, Charlene?"

She glanced up from her glass of red wine. "I can't tell," she said thoughtfully. "I used to be, but I think I got used to it. Maybe it's like getting fat. At first you're appalled that you gained the weight, then your eyes readjust to the mirror and you can't tell after a while if you're fat or not." Charlene is a classically slender brunette.

"You've never been fat in your life," I said.

"I know."

"And you're not fat now."

"Maybe I'm not lonely either."

I rolled my eyes at Joseph. Maybe solitude was damaging Charlene's brain.

"Don't *you* know anyone at work?" he asked me.

I concentrated. There *were* some heterosexual, unmarried men at work, but they didn't appeal to me. Therefore I had decided, in the classic manner of those who try to manipulate the universe, they would not appeal to Charlene either. But there was Tom, my boss's brother. He came in to have lunch with Laura every so often, and was very sweet. And Laura was giving a party to celebrate Don the Fascist's promotion next week, and Tom would probably be there.

I grinned widely. "Charlene, you and I are going to a party."

Joseph was taking a class the night of Laura's party, so Charlene and I were on our own. "Just like the old days," she said as we pushed into Laura's crowded house.

She meant pre-Joseph days, when we'd gone together to every party we could manage to get invited to, searching for Mr. Right. All we'd ever found, though, was Mr. Pâté and Mr. Gin and Tonic. I shuddered in recollection.

We greeted Laura and instinctively made our way to the food and drink.

"Hurray, sushi," Charlene said. "Hurray, champagne."

Charlene was more ruined than I'd realized—at this point, all a party meant to her was refreshment. She wasn't even looking at the men. And this was a shame because, working in advertising, I saw that they all looked somewhat like a magazine ad.

"Hurray, pâté and cornichons," Charlene continued, methodically eating her way to the end of the table like a depressed steamroller. Fortunately, at the end of the table stood Tom, looking as sweet as I remembered him. I introduced them.

"Tom works with the handicapped," I said brightly, having just recalled his profession. Oh good, I thought. They're both in social work. I knew this was a marriage made in heaven.

Tom was very shy. "Let me get you both more champagne," he said, taking our glasses and pursuing Laura. I turned to Charlene quickly. "You need to use the bathroom," I said. We used to say that to each other at parties when it seemed a good idea to comb hair and reapply lipstick.

"No, I don't," she said. We both reeked of cornichons.

Tom returned with our glasses refilled. "Charlene's in job development," I announced to him. He smiled; Charlene didn't. I drank hastily.

"Great food," I said.

"Laura's a fine hostess," he agreed. A man who likes his older sister is a good man indeed, I thought. And what sensitive, soulful brown eyes. Why wasn't Charlene talking to him? Why wasn't he asking her about her job? Why was he excusing himself to use the bathroom?

"Don't you think he's nice?" I insisted, when Tom had left the room.

But Charlene was pointing to a man in in the hallway. "Who's that?" she asked.

"The gayest man in San Francisco," I said. "Why?" I thought she was pointing to Darryl, Laura's secretary.

"No, I mean the blond."

"Oh. That's Don the Fascist. The guest of honor. He's the guy who got the promotion."

"Why do you call him a Fascist?"

"Because he is."

"He's handsome."

I squinted at Don. "In an Aryan kind of way, I guess."

"Introduce us."

I stared at her. "You want to meet Don the Fascist?" I asked, incredulous.

"Right after I use the bathroom."

She returned emanating toothpaste and Rive Gauche.

"He's a Republican," I warned.

"No one's perfect."

"He adores Bernie Goetz," I continued. Why didn't that sweet dark-haired Tom come back and put a stop to this?

"We're all entitled to our opinions," she said.

I gave up, introduced them, and proceeded to marvel at the change in Charlene's face. It became animated for the first time in two years. The flat tone of her voice suddenly found all sorts of peaks and valleys as she asked Don around six hundred questions about advertising—a line of work that I entered accidentally and about which, under normal circumstances, Charlene was barely polite.

My program had gone awry. Perhaps I could get it back on track. "Tell Don about your Lady Clairol experience," I urged Charlene, malevolently. Charlene had often delivered tirades about the evils of advertising as demonstrated by the Lady Clairol campaign of "Be A Blonde and See." Convinced at age nine that the brunette life was futile, she bleached her hair and it turned bright orange. Her mother had cut it all off, leaving her with an orange crewcut.

"I don't remember it," Charlene said.

"Let's sit down," Don suggested, leading Charlene away from me to a loveseat in the corner. He brought along pistachio nuts and a bottle of champagne too, in hopes, I surmised, that they'd never have to get up again. Wonderful, I thought. Charlene's setting up camp with a Fascist.

I retreated to another room just in time to see the brown-eyed Tom dancing with Darryl. My instincts really *are* off, I thought. I brooded for an hour, then returned to the living room to tell Charlene I was ready to leave. Laura informed me that she'd already left with Don twenty minutes ago.

=====

Joseph had no sympathy for me. "Charlene has a right to like anybody she wants," he said.

"She's a *social worker,*" I whined. "The most bleeding-heart liberal in the world. And Don's just slightly to the right of Attila the Hun."

"Opposites attract?"

"Not political opposites," I insisted.

"He's pretty rich, isn't he?"

"He's Mr. Investment. He's Mr. Success. It's all he ever talks about."

"And Charlene's family never had a dime," he said. He looked at me thoughtfully. "Did it ever occur to you that she might want to date a rich man for once? That she might want to get in on her fair share of expensive dinners and theater tickets?"

I envisioned Don and Charlene feasting on roast quail and Dom Perignon. "She wouldn't join the Nazi party just for a quail!" I protested.

"Hell hath no fury like a matchmaker scorned," he said, patting me on the head.

======

Don and Charlene were spending every weekend together. I knew about their plans, not because Charlene was confiding them to me, but because Don's office was three doors down the hall from mine. Whenever I walked by, I found myself listening for telltale phone conversations. When I stood before the message board, my gaze traveled more often than not from my designated corner to that of Don the Fascist. The pink "While You Were Out" slips piled up; they were calling each other often.

One afternoon I found myself dialing Charlene's work number. "Today's Friday," I said. "Want to be spontaneous and come eat pot roast at our house tonight?"

"Don's taking me to see *42nd Street* tonight."

Maybe Joseph was right; the tickets were astronomically priced.

"I thought you found musicals inane."

"We're seeing *The Lower Depths* tomorrow," she explained. "Fair exchange."

"Don? Gorki?"

"Don just needs the proper exposure."

What was she talking about—camera film or the most right-wing man in California? "Don's a Nazi," I said.

"Don's eyes are incredibly blue."

===

Joseph and I ate our pot roast alone. "I just can't understand her passing up that nice, sensitive Tom who devotes his life to helping the handicapped for that Fascist ex-surfer," I said.

"Tom's *gay,* for crissake!"

"So what? At least his politics are correct."

Joseph put down his fork. "Why does this irk you so much? Can't you just be glad that your best friend isn't lonely any more? Don't you want her to be happy?"

"Sure I do. I just wanted to pick the man that she'd be happy with."

"You want to manipulate the universe."

"So does everybody. At least I admit it."

===

Bringing Charlene to Laura's party had altered my life for the worse, and it was all my own fault. I missed Charlene and our pot roast dinners a lot. Joseph was wonderful, but he wasn't my girlfriend.

In addition, the atmosphere at work was rife with resentment. Don and I had always disliked each other, but mostly in a civilized, unarticulated fashion. Now it was open warfare. At conference meetings I'd catch him glaring at me with those evil blue eyes. I glared right back. Charlene was crazy—they weren't *that* blue. What did they see in each other? I wondered. They were natural enemies—oil and water, lion and gazelle. I called her.

"Why don't you and Don both come over for pot roast?" I asked. I couldn't believe I was extending this invitation, but I wanted to see them together and try to comprehend the attraction, even if it made me sick.

"You don't want Don in your home," Charlene scoffed.

"Sure I do," I lied. "Why not?"

"You hate him."

"I don't," I lied again.

She paused. "Well, he's not wild about you."

"Charlene," I pleaded. "What do you see in him?"

She giggled. "Remember sex?" she asked. Then she giggled again. I was furious.

$$=$$

"How can she abandon all her principles for some tawdry sex?" I asked Joseph. Every time I mentioned Charlene and Don, he tried to leave the room. I always followed him. "How can she be physically attracted to someone she's so philosophically opposed to in the first place?"

"Don't forget Kevin Everett," he taunted.

I'd forgotten I'd told him about Kevin Everett, the athletic, tanned, green-eyed president of my high school senior class. While I'd spent all my time in school reading Jack Kerouac and sending money to the Vietnam Day Committee, Kevin had campaigned for Nixon and wondered why everyone was so upset when Martin Luther King was shot. We hated each other. Ten years later at our high school reunion we fell into each other's arms with drunken lust. "I've wanted to sleep with you since we were fifteen," he'd whispered in my ear. I had never heard words more erotic. "Me, too!" I'd responded, finally admitting it to myself. I continued responding and admitting for the next seventy-two hours, at the end of which we exploded into a fight about food stamps. But up until that moment it had been passionate, exquisite, an erotic dream fulfilled.

I blushed. "Never mind Kevin Everett," I said.

Joseph smirked and sat down to grade papers.

$$=$$

I was behaving badly, but I couldn't help myself. I brought Gloria Steinem's *Outrageous Acts and Everyday Rebellions* to the office and left it on my desk so that Don would see it and be irritated.

I also tried the countertechnique of diverting Charlene with other men.

"Joseph has a brother, you know," I told her. "He likes pot roast. Why don't the four of us have dinner together?"

"His brother is twenty-two years old," Charlene said. I was hoping she forgot.

"He's cute, even cuter than Joseph," I urged. "And very bright."

"He's too young. I don't want to be Blanche DuBois."

"Better than Eva Braun."

"That's not fair! You don't really know Don."

"I've worked in the same office with him for five years. I know him. Look, Charlene, be honest. This is a Kevin Everett sort of thing, isn't it?" She'd attended the same high school reunion and knew the whole embarrassing story.

"It's far more complicated," she said.

"Sex isn't complicated, it's simple and basic."

"Sex is incredibly complicated. And anyway, it isn't just sex. Don needs me."

"You're talking like a social worker."

"I am a social worker."

"You're working on a hopeless case."

"No, I'm not."

"What about my dentist?" I asked suddenly. "He's single, and he has lovely hands. I could invite him for pot roast—I'm having a check-up tomorrow."

"My teeth are perfect," she said, and hung up.

═══

I stopped trying to find other men for Charlene; in fact, I vowed never to be a matchmaker again. What I didn't stop was trying to annoy Don. I planted Marilyn French novels at strategic points of the office. I taped an antinuke flyer to the water cooler.

"That was a good book," Don said to me one morning, sticking his head inside my office, something that in the entire five years we'd worked together he had never done. "I hope you don't mind my borrowing it."

I was so surprised I actually felt weak. I clutched my coffee mug for support. "What book?" I asked.

"That Steinem thing. She's pretty smart."

"You hate Gloria Steinem!" I said. At least he did two years ago when we'd had an altercation about her in the conference room.

"That was a long time ago," he said.

"Two years is not a long time," I said, as his head disappeared. I stared into my coffee cup; time is relative, I thought. Maybe for blonds two years is like a decade.

The next week Don came to work without wearing a tie. "What are you—a drug-crazed hippie?" I asked him. He had never come in without a tie and wing tips.

"Maybe," he said affably. He was holding a paperback copy of Gorki's *Lower Depths.* I stared at it. "Charlene took me to see this," he explained.

"So I heard," I mumbled. Charlene was either the best lover in the world or the best social worker. Could sex make a man change his politics?

I shut my office door and called her. "Do you have some erotic secrets you haven't told me about?" I asked. "What's your technique? What makes you so powerful?"

She laughed. "I don't have any secret powers."

"You are in the process of changing Don the Fascist. You *must* have powers."

"Don the Fascist was ready to change himself. That's why he liked me. You know you can't change anyone."

Right. Trying to change someone was like trying to manipulate the universe. Not possible.

"I miss you," I told her. "Can't we forget about Joseph and Don and get together for a drink?"

"Absolutely. Don's doing our laundry tonight, so I'm free. Let's meet at six."

Don doing the laundry. Even the egalitarian Joseph always managed to squirm out of that one. Lucky Charlene. All that and money too.

Charlene was radiant while we shared our wine. She almost glistened with well-being, talking about Don happily but, I noted, not obsessively. I apologized for torturing Don and invited them again for a pot roast dinner. This time she graciously accepted.

"Do you think we could make it a sixsome?" she asked. "My little sister is looking for a boyfriend, and she's just twenty-one. I thought maybe I could bring her and Joseph could invite his brother and we could just see what happened."

For a moment my old impulse was deliriously reactivated, but only for a moment. It was comforting to know that Charlene and I shared the same affliction: as soon as she felt happy with someone, she wanted to share the wealth.

"I think four people is all I can handle," I said. "And I'm not even sure I can handle that."

Charlene laughed. She understood. "We'll have a good time," she assured me. "We won't mention sex, politics, or religion."

"And we'll drink moderately."

"And we'll enjoy—quietly—the best pot roast ever cooked in the western world."

6. Puppy Love

I met Perry, an athletic redhead, and Babe, his loyal Samoyed, at the same time. Perry was taking Babe for her evening stroll, their destination the same as mine: the VCR rental store. Babe stood outside leashed to a parking meter, while Perry and I joined all the other young professionals seeking video relief from a dateless Saturday night. I chose *The Women* so I could once again hear the Countess De Lave shriek the words: *"L'amour! L'amour! How it *can* let you down!"*, a high point in American cinema. Perry selected *Lassie Come Home.*

We left the store at the same moment, and I couldn't help commenting on Babe, who is platinum-haired and voluptuous looking—sort of a Jean Harlow dog. "What a beautiful animal," I said. "Do you show her professionally?"

Perry scratched Babe's white head. "No, she hates public life. Don't you, Babe?"

Babe barked her agreement and, unleashed from the meter, fell into step with Perry, who had fallen into step with me. "Live around here?" he asked.

"Five blocks up," I said.

"I'm just around the corner. I've never seen you in the neighborhood."

"I just moved in."

This news brought forth all his recommendations on the local merchants: Blake's dry cleaning was better than Sunshine's; Caselli's delicatessen had the best chopped liver in the city, and would I like to come up to his apartment for a drink?

"I just met you. Which local bar serves the best drinks?" I asked, thinking myself extremely diplomatic.

"The Mainline does," he said, indicating a trendy place across the street, but not moving toward it.

"Well?"

He hesitated. "It's just that I hate to tie Babe up for that long."

I thought Babe was a ploy to get me inside his apartment, and I hadn't read *Looking for Mr. Goodbar* for nothing. "Well, good night then," I said pleasantly.

He vacillated. Babe sniffed a mailbox. I put my cassette in my purse. "What the hell," he said. "Let's go have a drink."

Living alone in a new neighborhood, I'd have considered drinking with the street cleaner if he'd asked, but he hadn't. So I shared a half carafe of Chablis with Perry, who turned out to be a divorced tax lawyer who liked basketball and seafood. His hands were strong and freckled, his eyes big and brown. He was lovely to look at.

"Do you live alone now?" I asked, not meaning to sound like Barbara Walters, but curious.

"No, I live with Babe."

I briefly wondered, as we exchanged business cards, if that meant Babe paid part of the rent. An uncanny bark sounded outside the Mainline's door.

"Well, gotta go," Perry said. "Nice meeting you—I'll give you a call."

And so we parted—he to spend the evening with Lassie and Babe, I to commune with Joan Crawford and Rosalind Russell—bitches, I thought, of a much higher order.

Perry and I worked near each other, and Monday morning he called to ask me to lunch.

"Fine, I'll meet you at your office," I volunteered. If I can see for myself that a man wears a suit in an actual office where his name is on the stationery, I am somewhat reassured that he probably isn't an axe murderer.

The receptionist showed me a seat in Perry's office, explaining that he'd be back in a minute. I assessed his desk; sure enough, his name was on the stationery. A framed photograph stood beside his letter opener. His ex-wife? Unmentioned children? Glancing quickly at the door, I flipped the photo toward me and saw the smiling muzzle of Babe. I turned it back just as Perry walked in. "Ready for lunch?" he asked.

"Sure!" So he's fond of his dog, I thought. At least he's not a killer.

Lunch went so well that Perry invited me to his apartment for dinner that Friday, a gesture that always charms me. If men knew how happy women are to eat even a tuna sandwich prepared by male hands, they'd never leave the kitchen.

Grateful in advance, I brought wine, flowers, and a box of doggie biscuits for Babe. Perry and Babe had been together for the three years since his divorce (perhaps since Babe's too—I did not know her marital status); if I'm nice to Babe, I reasoned, Perry will be nice to me.

The doggie biscuits impressed Perry as much as his dinner invitation impressed me. "You must be a real dog lover," he said, as we sat on his couch sipping wine. Babe sat at Perry's feet while he scratched her head.

"Oh, sure. I love dogs," I said. I have known perhaps four dogs in my life and never owned one, but I liked them well enough. Why not?

"Babe's the best dog in the world," he said, his deep brown eyes aglow. "Aren't ya, girl?" he said to Babe, who yipped happily.

If I lay at Perry's feet, I wondered if he'd scratch *my* head. That would feel nice, I thought, sipping more wine.

I wasn't planning to sleep with Perry on the first date, but I changed my mind for several reasons: (1) It wasn't really our first date, it was our third, counting the drink at the Mainline and lunch downtown; (2) He served broiled lobster for dinner; (3) I am no longer influenced by songs like The Shirelles' "Will You Still Love Me Tomorrow"; and finally, (4) Perry was an absolutely first-rate kisser.

Knowing it was too early in the game to wash off my makeup before going to sleep, I blissfully passed out with a dirty face. When I woke up, an eighty-pound weight paralyzed my right leg, and I found myself staring into a pair of soulful brown eyes—not Perry's, but Babe's.

Her morning breath was devastating. I tried to read her expression but had no idea what facial expressions a dog is capable of, let alone what they might mean. "Nice dog," I whispered, reaching to scratch behind her ears as Perry softly snored. Babe deftly averted her head.

"Be that way," I whispered, yanking a robe from an armchair and heading for the living room, where I'd left my purse and most of my clothes. Hopefully I could repair my makeup before Perry awoke and decided our encounter was all a hideous mistake.

I followed a trail of lobster shells and wineglasses to my purse, which had evidently exploded on the couch. My makeup bag was particularly violated—the contents scattered, pounced upon, bitten, smeared.

I was halfway under a chair retrieving a lipstick when Perry spoke.

"What are you doing?" he asked from the doorway.

"I think Babe got into my purse last night."

"She wouldn't do that."

I hoped he wouldn't notice that I had mascara on my chin. "Well, *someone* did," I said, attempting a light tone. God, he had a nice torso. He was wearing jeans and running shoes and was pulling on a shirt. "Where are you going?" I asked from the floor, heartbroken to see his chest disappear.

"Babe's morning walk."

Babe didn't look at me as she led Perry out the front door, skipping in perverse canine triumph. I scrambled for the rest of my makeup, showered, repaired my face and returned to Perry's bed. I plumped up the pillows and leafed through the morning paper. When Perry came back, I would appear willing, but not voracious.

"Breakfast?" I heard him shout forty-five minutes later from the kitchen.

"What?" I shouted back. I hoped he'd come into the bedroom to repeat the proposition and notice there was something better to do than eat breakfast.

"Breakfast," he shouted again. Everyone in the apartment building heard it, so I couldn't pretend I didn't.

So he doesn't like morning sex, I thought, putting his robe back on. He's still not an axe murderer.

I invited Perry for dinner the following weekend; I do not recall inviting Babe. Still, there she stood at my door alongside her dashing, auburn-haired master.

"Oh dear, I don't have anything for her to eat," I said, trying to look at once desirable and forlorn.

"That's okay, I brought her dinner." He was equipped with a can of Alpo, a bottle of white Zinfandel, and a bowl labeled "Babe."

"I guess you thought of everything," I said with forced cheer. Then he kissed me and the cheer became authentic.

Babe slurped Alpo in the kitchen while Perry and I held hands and fed each other halibut in tarragon sauce. Restless in her new surroundings, she quickly finished her dinner and tried to lay her head in Perry's lap. This was not easy, because my left foot was already there. She then sniffed the halibut and whined.

I stifled the urge to tell her not to beg—wasn't that Perry's job? To reprimand another person's pet is like presuming to discipline someone else's children. I smiled sweetly at Babe and asked, "Does she want a taste?"

"Oh, God, no—this food would make her sick!" Perry said vehemently.

"Would it?" I kept smiling.

"You know what I mean. The spices and all." He kissed the top of Babe's head. "And we don't want a sick girl on our hands, do we, Babe?" He nuzzled her.

A sick girl on his hands was just what Perry was about to have, I thought, continuing to smile.

———

My bedroom door was closed, and Perry was once again convincing me that the smartest move I'd ever made was to this neighborhood, when Babe began to whine outside the door.

"Do you mind if we let her in?" he asked.

"Well, actually, yes. I think it would make me self-conscious."

"She's just a dog. She doesn't know what we're doing."

"But *I* know what we're doing, and I'd rather we did it without being watched."

He laughed. "Babe won't watch! She doesn't care that we're making love."

"Then why does she want to come in here?"

"She's lonely."

"I was lonely for a whole year once. I didn't try to break into people's bedrooms."

Perry scratched his head. "Really? You were lonely for a year? You should have bought yourself a dog."

"I don't think a dog would keep me from being lonely."

"Oh, you're wrong. A dog is wonderful company."

"I'm sure that's true, but I like to *talk* to someone."

"I talk to Babe all the time."

"Well, I need the someone to talk *back.*"

"Babe talks back. Listen—she's talking now." The whines were increasing. In fact, she was starting to wail.

"Please, Perry, please let Babe sleep in the hall."

"You're cute when you're worried," he said, and kissed me in that clever way he had. He proceeded to do all sorts of wonderful things. I proceeded to lose my mind, and an hour later Babe was sleeping at the foot of my bed.

In the morning I woke to Perry's tender voice saying, "Did you sleep well, Babe?"

"Oh yes, sweetheart," I murmured, reaching for him—but he hadn't been addressing me.

In no time they were up and ready for Babe's morning romp. "Want to join us?" Perry asked.

A romp through the fog at 8 o'clock Sunday morning? No, thanks. I went back to sleep and dreamed about *Old Yeller,* the Disney movie in which the beloved family dog had died.

=====

Perry and I remained in that romantic twilight zone that has always caused me untold stress—the phase before any declarations are made. Not that I assumed any declarations *would* be made; I knew that for Perry my greatest attraction might well be my proximity. He was not my boyfriend; he was merely someone with whom I shared meals, beds and double bills at the Metro. For all I knew, he was sharing these things with six other women on a rotating schedule. Although each time we parted I felt sure I'd see him again soon, I had no idea when.

Soon I decided I wanted Perry to tell me he loved me, so I could start becoming self-righteous and territorial. If I couldn't have that, I wanted a monthly calendar with our dating schedule inked in. I can stand anything except uncertainty. Correction: uncertainty and canine animosity.

Once Babe had ascertained that I wasn't just a one-night stand, she dropped all pretense of being a civilized dog. She hated me in a covert, calculated style designed to elude Perry and torture me. The makeup bag explosion happened three more times before I learned to keep my purse in Perry's refrigerator.

"Babe resents me," I told Perry one morning when she had once again swept my scrambled eggs onto the floor with one swift flick of her bushy white tail.

"Hey, it was an accident," he said, hugging the pouting pet.

"You bitch!" I hissed at her, when Perry had gone to get more coffee. She launched into a vicious growl that died the moment he reappeared.

"It's important that you and Babe be friends," Perry said, gallantly sharing his eggs with me. "You're the two most important women in my life."

"We are?" I said, trying to conceal some of my vast pleasure. If you ignored the implications of being accorded equal status with a dog, Perry's remark came very close to being a declaration. There are many ways for a man to say "I love you"; I think I've analyzed them all.

I became dewy-eyed. Perry even became a little dewy-eyed. Befitting this sentimental moment, we returned to his bedroom, shutting the door firmly on Babe's cold wet nose. Feeling territorial already, I not only shut the door; I locked it.

At least there was *one* area in which Babe was no competition.

═══

"Maybe you should register Babe at Doggie's Talent Agency," I suggested to Perry one evening, while looking through a magazine. "See these dogs they use for advertisements? You could make a lot of money." My hope was that Babe would be discovered by Hollywood and have to move south to promote her career.

"Babe doesn't want to work for a living, do you, girl?" he said, patting her vigorously.

I mouthed the words "dumb blonde" so that only Babe could see me.

"Maybe she could teach English overseas, then. Or join the Peace Corps. Or tour Europe. Has she ever been?" I laughed. Perry laughed. Babe glared.

"You've got a great sense of humor," Perry told me.

Right, I was a laugh a minute. Babe had chewed up five pairs of my shoes, my wallet with all my identification, and the one stuffed animal I'd saved from childhood, a beatup bunny named Bun. It was the murder of dear Bun that distressed me the most.

"It's weird—she never touches my things," Perry said.

"That's because she doesn't hate you."

"Come on, why should Babe hate you? Dogs aren't capable of hatred."

I thought of Bun's brutalized little body, her pathetic stuffing strewn all over my bedroom. "Well, Babe is! She hates me because she's jealous! She wants you all to herself."

"Relax. Babe's a dog, remember, not a person."

"You treat her like a person. You treat her better than a person." Better than *this* person, I meant, thinking of my neglected self. Why was Perry so cute? Why was his hair the color of an autumn leaf? Why did he have to be in love with his dog?

═══

"It's probably psychosomatic," the allergy doctor told me after inspecting the angry red hives that covered my body. I had given her a detailed account of my feelings for Perry and for Babe, the murder of Bun, the overturned breakfasts.

"You mean it's all in my head?" I sneezed. I'd been sneezing for a week, and I didn't have a cold.

"Well, it began in your head, but now it's in your body."

"How do I treat it?"

"You must resolve the conflict."

"You mean kill Babe?" I had often suggested to Babe that she play in traffic.

The doctor was patient. "No, don't kill the dog. Just stay away from her."

Stay away from Babe? That meant staying away from Perry. Unless Perry stayed away from Babe, too.

"This means Perry has to choose between us, doesn't it?"

She was writing a prescription for anti-itch lotion. "Good luck, dear," she said, handing me the slip of paper.

My heart was in my throat that night when I called to tell Perry I was allergic to Babe. Just as I have studied the many ways men declare love, so have I studied the many ways they sabotage intimacy. Babe was the most inventive barrier I'd yet encountered.

"A real, actual allergy?" Perry asked. "Is that what the doctor said?"

"You've seen my body," I said.

"Not recently enough."

Oh, good. "Well, come over and see it. But you'll have to leave Babe at home. Doctor's orders."

He came right over, saw and celebrated my body, and then could not fall asleep. "I keep thinking of Babe being all alone."

"I'm alone five nights a week," I reminded him. "She'll adjust." I scratched my arm, then my leg. Just the mention of Babe exacerbated my condition.

"I hope she isn't frightened."

Were dogs afraid of axe murderers, too? "She's probably asleep," I said. Or planning my demise, I thought. "We should be asleep, too."

At 3:00 A.M. I awoke to find Perry up and dressed. "I'm sorry," he said. "I just have to check up on her."

I've lost men to their consuming careers, to their love of alcohol, and even once to the proverbial blonde. But never before to a dog. "Perry?" I whispered.

"Yeah?" He was turning the doorknob.

"Don't bother coming back."

He looked at me as if he didn't believe I was serious. I almost didn't believe I was either, until I woke seven hours later and saw that my hives had all disappeared. The phone rang three times, and I didn't answer it. I made breakfast. No one knocked it to the floor. Somewhere in the neighborhood a dog was barking. I closed the window to shut out the noise.

I wondered, as I ate my eggs, read the paper, and ignored the ringing phone, if *The Thin Man* would be available at the VCR rental store that night; an old movie always made me feel better.

Then I remembered the character of Asta—the clever white terrier belonging to Nick and Nora Charles—and decided to go with *Casablanca* instead.

7. Adult Education

David pulled my novel out of my hands and replaced it with the community college catalog. It was opened to page nine, where a listing for a Tuesday night fiction workshop was circled in red ink. "I'll sign up if you do," David said.

David and I took writing classes together in college; our friendship grew out of the mutual humiliation of hearing our short stories read aloud in class. The most torturous course was taught by Professor White, who used words like "trivial" and "obvious" to critique our work. After class David and I would get off campus as quickly as possible and head for the nearest beer. "We'll never be writers," we'd lament over our icy beer mugs. By the end of sophomore year we'd dispensed with our dreams of writing and moved on to more practical endeavors.

"Why in the world would you want to take this class?" I asked David now. "All you've written since college are legal briefs."

David adjusted his horn-rimmed glasses. "I want to meet women," he said. "And that's what adult education is all about —meeting intelligent women."

"So why should *I* take the class?"

"To meet intelligent men."

"Why do we want to do that?"

"Because we can't spend the rest of our lives cooking dinner for each other and watching reruns of *Dallas*."

David had accurately described our routine of the past two months. Our respective romantic lives had fizzled out within weeks of each other, inciting a renewal of our old platonic friendship—asexual and comforting.

"I don't think I want to meet men," I said. Watching J. R. Ewing was enough for me. Did I have to try to date him, too?

"But I want to meet women. The only woman I know right now besides you is my secretary, and if I date her my office life will be a mess. If we enroll together, it could be fun."

"Meaning you don't want to do it alone."

"Right."

I read the course description again. "It costs a hundred and fifty dollars," I said.

"It's an investment in your future."

"I can't afford it," I said, tossing the catalog aside.

"You can if I pay for it."

David, though not cheap, isn't exactly free with his money; this offer signaled true desperation. "I'm exhausted after working all day," I said. "I don't want to go to a night class." I picked up the catalog again. "It goes till ten P.M., for God's sake."

"You are such a couch potato! A night class is exactly what you need—it will get you out of the house."

I looked at David. He looked at me. Behind his oversized glasses his eyes were pleading. "All right," I said. He beamed. "There's just one thing," I said.

"What? I said I'd pay."

"It's not that. It's the class itself. We'll have to *write* something. Did you forget that part?"

He unbeamed just slightly. "We'll worry about that when the time comes."

———

David not only paid my enrollment fee, he bought each of us a spiral notebook with a shiny red cover and an extra-fine felt-tip pen. He also promised to drive us back and forth to all ten sessions.

"I still don't understand why you picked *this* course," I told him en route to the first class. "Don't you remember how hideous it was in freshman year? Writing courses aren't easy. I think we should have picked something easy." I tried to think what that might be, and came up with nothing. I remembered that I basically hated being a student. Once I'd gotten my degree, I'd thrilled to the idea of leaving the world of study and final exams forever. Life was tolerable, I'd thought, only if you never had to write another paper.

The moment we located our classroom, I knew why David had picked creative writing. Eighty percent of the students were women.

"Men take stuff like accounting," he explained, as we found two chairs in the back of the room.

"Good, I'll transfer."

He grabbed my wrist. "You can't. I paid the fee and our contract was that you'd stay with me," he said in his most lawyer-like way.

"There are three men in here!" I whined.

"So what? You didn't want to meet them anyway."

I sighed, arranging my styrofoam coffee cup and oatmeal cookie carefully on my desk. At least the instructor was male and, thank God, was not Professor White hired to plague me ten years later. Professor Charles Slade was Southern, sucked on a pipe and wore an anachronistic gray suit. I have always found pipes an offensive affectation, and especially so in the mouths of professors.

"Have any of you ever published a short story?" Professor Slade asked, after informing us that he had, and often.

No one had. David's relieved sigh was audible. I swallowed my own.

The pipe, when not in the professor's mouth, made circles in the air. "Can any of you tell me which writers you enjoy reading?"

I didn't speak up once in four years of college and I was not about to break my vow of academic silence. David raised his hand.

"Flannery O'Connor," he said.

I sneered at him and scribbled in the margin of my spiral notebook: "Southern for teacher, female for the ladies. Good work."

David sneered back and helped himself to half my oatmeal cookie. I felt as if I was in junior high. Would Professor Slade catch us passing notes and reprimand us in front of the class? Were we allowed to eat sweets? I guessed that, for $150, we could do anything we liked. Maybe I'd put gum on David's seat when he got up to sharpen his pencil.

A pretty, black-haired woman with extravagant earrings said she liked Eudora Welty. Professor Slade approved.

David approved even more. "She looks like a flamenco dancer," he whispered as we stood in the hall during the break.

"Does this mean you've met your intelligent woman?"

"Don't be snide. I'm paying for this, you know."

"So you keep reminding me. To think I could be watching Bobby and Pamela trying to patch up their marriage."

We returned to class at the appointed time and, instead of taking his original seat in the back, David slid past me and into the seat next to Ms. Flamenco.

I was momentarily flustered.

"This one's available," drawled Professor Slade, waving his pipe toward a seat almost directly in front of him.

Helpless, I sat down. I'd always avoided the front row because you have to look attentive, and you have to take real notes because the instructor can saunter by and read them, if his vision is good. I jotted diligently as Professor Slade nattered on about less being more and showing being preferable to telling.

"It's nine-thirty," he suddenly announced, just as I was about to nod off. "We'll end the class now because it's our first session and we've nothing to critique. Please bring a story next Tuesday. Ten typed double-spaced pages will be fine." I gathered my coat and notebook and stood up. The professor blocked my path.

"It's still early," he drawled, consulting his watch as if he hadn't just done so. "May I interest you in a drink?"

A vision flashed in my head: Abigail Grossman, a college classmate who'd had an affair with Professor Tim Keen, our Romantic Poetry teacher. It was the talk of the campus. I'd been appalled and slightly envious; Abigail was so cool. So adult. So naughty.

"Uh . . . I'm with him," I stuttered, pointing to David. "I mean, he's driving me home. Thanks."

"Professor Slade, excuse me." Flamenco was tugging on his arm. "I have to tell you—your *Mimosa Madness* is my absolutely favorite novel in this world." David was right behind her.

Professor Slade's drawl grew a trifle lazier, sweeter. "Thank you, dear," he said. "Shall we all go down the street for a drink?"

"Oh, yes!" said David and Flamenco simultaneously. David smiled at Flamenco, who smiled at Professor Slade, who smiled at me.

"Sure, I could use a drink," I said, defeated. To think I could have been watching Sue Ellen battling her addiction to alcohol.

=====

"She's beautiful," David said as we drove home, referring to Flamenco, whose real name was Betsy Cohen. "Her hair is so black, it's almost blue. Like Veronica Lodge in *Archie* comics, remember?"

"Betsy has a crush on the teacher," I said. "I couldn't believe it when he ordered a bourbon and branch. Just like J. R."

"Can't you stop thinking about *Dallas?*" He sped up in exasperation. "Help me think of a way to make Betsy like me."

"Speak in a Southern accent. Order bourbon."

"Be serious."

"*You* be serious. You took this class to meet intelligent, well-educated women. Betsy's a stewardess."

"Don't be such a snob. Stewardesses are smart."

"I'm sure they are. But Betsy uses double negatives."

"Only once."

"Okay, she's Madame Curie. But she still likes Professor Slade and not you."

David sulked and drove with equal concentration. I let him sulk for three minutes, then said, "I can prove Betsy's stupid."

"How?"

"She liked *Mimosa Madness.*"

To his credit, David laughed. "She's still beautiful," he said.

====

Colonel Slade, as David and I were now calling him, phoned me Saturday to suggest we have dinner Tuesday night before class.

"With David and Betsy?" I asked.

"No, just the two of us. Am I scaring you?"

In fact, he was. "Oh, gee," I said. I did not want to dine with the Colonel, but I didn't know how to get out of it. I go everywhere I'm asked because I've never known how to get out of it.

"I'd like to discuss your writing projects with you," he drawled.

Wonderful—my grocery lists? My thank-you notes?

"I'll pick you up at five-thirty," he said.

"You don't know where I live," I said, thinking that maybe I'd found a way out of it.

"Your address is on the class roster, my dear."

====

The Colonel was on his third bourbon and branch when our spaghetti carbonara arrived. "So tell me," he said, his tongue flickering in true William F. Buckley tradition. "Are you handing in a short story tonight?"

I shook my head. "I have writer's block."

"That's a terrible shame," he said, furrowing his brow. "How long have you had it?"

"Oh, at least six months. I took this class to try to conquer it," I said, frenetically blanketing my pasta with a pound of parmesan. Damn David, I thought.

The Colonel took my hand. "There's cheese already in it. Now, about this writer's block." He held onto my hand. "We need to find a way to get those creative juices flowing again." He gave the words "juices" and "flowing" about thirty syllables each.

"We do?"

"Indeed we do. I'm sure a lady like you has a great deal to say and can say it eloquently, once she isn't blocked."

Professor White didn't think so, I thought.

"You need to break down those rigid defenses," he continued, pouring me more Burgundy. "You need to succumb to the Muse."

I did? Did Abigail Grossman succumb? Did she at least get an "A" from Professor Keen?

"I am quite familiar with the evils of writer's block," Slade said, his vowels wading through molasses. "I know I can help you. You must promise to let me help you."

Must I? I withdrew my hand and started buttering bread like a madwoman. I wondered if it was too late to transfer to Beginning Auto Shop.

=====

We got to class with two minutes to spare. I sat in the back, directly behind the biggest person I could find, a burly truck-driver type who was working on a novel. David had moved his seat so close to Betsy's he was almost smashing her into the wall.

"Any stories this evening?" the Colonel asked, perching himself on the corner of his desk and lighting up his pipe.

No one moved.

"Come now, we can't all be suffering from writer's block." He chuckled, giving me a significant glance. David caught the glance and looked at me. I smiled and mouthed the words "Damn you" in his direction.

Betsy, wearing a red hat, red dress, and red shoes, walked shyly to the front of the room and handed the Colonel a paper-clipped manuscript.

"Thank you, my dear," he said, dropping it on the desk. She remained standing there. She was, I figured, either overwhelmed with the courage of her own action, or simply making sure the Colonel absorbed the full impact of her redness.

"Thank you, Betsy," he said. This time she walked back to her seat. David nearly renovated the room clearing her way.

"Any others?" he asked. Again, no one moved.

Reluctantly, he withdrew his pipe and rustled the pages of Betsy's story. "Well, then, I shall read to you a story the writer calls 'Love Above the Clouds.' "

The title was the least distressing element of Betsy's tale about a well-meaning stewardess and a smooth-talking corporate executive in first class who manages to seduce her an hour before landing. The erotic aspect consisted mostly of a clumsy string of observations about the awkward confines of airplane restrooms. As I listened, I drew pictures of airplanes in my notebook, wishing I were somewhere else. Perhaps in Auto Shop. Or Dallas.

"Do we have any comments on this . . . intriguing piece of work?" the Colonel asked, finally able to resume chomping on his pipe.

David's arm shot into the air. "I thought it was brilliant. Just brilliant. Such sensitivity. Such powerful dialogue." He proceeded to recite the cover blurb of every paperback novel he'd ever seen.

A woman wearing a green kilt raised her hand. "Doesn't the writer have a small cliché problem?" she hesitantly asked.

"A small one, yes," conceded the Colonel. Betsy's head was on her desk, her coal-black tresses spilling over its edges.

"I don't agree," bellowed David. I slumped further into my seat.

"You're awfully quiet back there," the Colonel said, waving his pipe toward my corner of the room. "Do you have any helpful criticisms to offer?" He meant me.

"Me?" I said stupidly, straightening up. "Oh, gee. Oh, gee— I think we could all use some coffee, don't you?"

========

All the way home I berated David mercilessly. "Just brilliant!" I mocked him. "Such powerful dialogue!"

"Well, it wasn't that bad."

"Are you kidding?"

"She writes pretty well about sex."

"In your condition, you'd think anybody wrote pretty well about sex."

"That's true. So what? How's your writer's block, anyway?" He chortled. "Writer's block. I can't believe you told the Colonel you had writer's block."

"It's not such a bad affliction. Betsy should be so lucky."

Three days later Colonel Slade called and asked me, once again, to dinner. This time he suggested a late supper after class, giving us unlimited time to stimulate my juices.

I accepted, not because I wanted to go or because I couldn't think of a way out, but because David and I had a master plan that would hopefully terminate Colonel Slade's dinner invitations forever while sending Betsy flying to David's arms. Actually, the idea was David's. "It's a fiction workshop, right?" he reasoned. "So we should achieve our goals through the art of fiction. You should write a story about a loathsome character who smokes a pipe, and I should write one about a goddess flamenco dancer. Colonel Slade will stop bothering you, and Betsy will be flattered into giving me her phone number."

"I'll get a bad grade," I said.

"We're both signed up on a non-credit basis," he said. "Don't worry."

We sat down with our spiral notebooks, felt-tip pens and beer, and tried to write. Tentative scribbles, then silence, more scribbles, more silence. "I think I'd rather write about the flamenco dancer," I said.

"Great idea!" said David, pushing his glasses back up the bridge of his nose. "We'll write each other's stories. I know I can write a great Southern dialect."

"You're making him Southern, too?"

"Oh, yeah. Let's go all the way."

"Can't I be sued for libel?"

"It won't be *published.*"

"All right." Our pens started to fly. So did the time. Two hours later we were both finished. "Let's read them aloud," I suggested.

"No, let's make this really interesting. We'll type up our stories, put each other's name on it, and turn it in Tuesday night. The first time we'll hear 'our' work will be when the Colonel reads it."

"That's scary."

"Gutless couch potato."

That did it. "You're on," I said.

The next week David and I drove to class, basking in the serenity of a student who has completed his assignment and done a good job. Of course, we didn't actually know how good a job we'd done.

"You described Betsy as the perfect woman, didn't you?" he asked, slightly anxious. "No snotty stewardess remarks?"

"She's a combination of Helen of Troy and Eleanor Roosevelt."

"Great. I knew I could count on you. And don't worry about your story—I creamed the Colonel."

"I have no doubt."

We turned into the parking lot and were looking for a space when David suddenly stopped the car. "Isn't that the Colonel's Mazda?"

"I don't know if it's his car, but he's certainly in it," I said. "I'd recognize that pipe anywhere."

The Colonel sat in the driver's seat, with Betsy arranged oddly on his lap in an embrace that looked as if it could be painlessly accomplished only by someone trained in airplane restrooms.

"I think he's helping her get unblocked," I said.

"Are they crazy? It's still daylight! Everyone can see them."

"They're succumbing to the Muse."

Betsy's black hair traveled from one end of the car to the other. Colonel Slade's pipe flew into the back seat.

"That's *real* passion," I observed.

"This is horrible," David said. I felt sorry for him. He'd really believed that Betsy was Eleanor Roosevelt.

"Let's stop watching," I suggested, patting him on the shoulder.

"Adult education stinks!" he yelled, backing the car out of the lot. He sped down the street while I yelled at him to calm down.

"What are we going to do now?" he asked.

I pointed to a corner grocery store. "We're going to stop here and buy some wine and some dinner, go to your house, get drunk, read our stories, and watch a *Dallas* rerun."

David was too crushed to resist my plan. We were fortunate that it turned out to be the episode of *Dallas* wherein J. R. got shot. We pretended J. R. was Colonel Slade and laughed until we cried.

8. Frito Pie: Love with a Restaurant Critic

I won't say that Ben Hamilton's being a restaurant critic was the only reason I dated him. It was, however, the main one. And why not? They say you can fall for a rich man as easily as for a poor one; I say you can be as attracted to a man who has endless access to fabulous free meals as to one who frequents Burger King.

Opportunistic? Yes. Did I use Ben so I could go to Masa's without making reservations six weeks in advance? Absolutely. Call me what you will—like Edith Piaf, I regret nothing. If Ben suffered because of me, it was certainly no more than when his lamb was overcooked. And I myself suffered a far more serious upheaval: I lost my lifelong love of fine food. And how am I convinced of this loss? Because I have just polished off a big bowlful of Kraft's Macaroni and Cheese. Because, far worse, I have enjoyed it.

I had read Ben's newspaper column for years, just as every restaurant-crazed resident of our city has. He has the power to make or break a new eatery with the stroke of his pen. Every Wednesday I turned straight to his byline and devoured reports of festive evenings with feasting friends. Even more seductive than his accounts of duck breast with green peppercorns were the intimations of conviviality: "The five of us agreed that no appe-

tizer on the menu could match the leek pâté with tarragon sauce."
"Although more than satiated, our group shared a pear-and-ginger
tart and a chocolate orange soufflé, unanimously deeming the tart
the superior dessert."

I lusted for such pastimes as this: to luxuriate with my knowl-
edgeable peers in this cocoon of fine food and wine, to share
tender judgments, to evaluate, to discuss nothing more controver-
sial than pear versus chocolate. "I belong at that table!" I'd reflect
as I read. I'd even bring my own notepad, and I would know
immediately if the escargots had Pernod in them or not.

Actually, I had never dreamed I'd be so lucky as to meet Mr.
Haute Cuisine, just as I have never dreamed of meeting Elvis
Presley or Mick Jagger. He came to me, as miracles do, unan-
nounced. I stood alone at an elaborate cocktail party beside a
gleaming chafing dish, and he walked up and introduced himself.

Did I panic and wish I had just freshened my lipstick? Did I
wish I hadn't just put a run in my stocking? No. I wished more
than anything in the world that I was not in the middle of
consuming a cold prawn dipped in mustard vinaigrette. I could
still hear him railing in his latest column against the omnipresence
of the prawn: "Are these crustaceans not the most ubiquitous of
all? Can hosts not think of more imaginative fare?"

"Forgive me," I said quickly, nervously depositing the uneaten
half of my prawn into a pitcher of aioli sauce. "Oh, God." I
retrieved it clumsily and wrapped its nasty pinkness in a napkin.
"Forgive me," I mumbled.

"There is nothing to forgive," he said generously. He was four
inches shorter than I, with blazing brown eyes. "Try this," he said,
slipping a scallop adorned with fresh cilantro into my mouth.
"Better?"

Having received the communal Host, I was again pure. "Thank
you," I murmured, as he fed me another one. Twice blessed. "I
read your column every week," I blurted.

"That's very good of you," he said. "And may I say that your dress is quite lovely? It is precisely the color of an eggplant."

Imagine Priscilla Presley's joy when the King of Rock and Roll chose her, from all the corners of the universe, to be his bride. Imagine mine.

"Do you fear innards?" Ben then asked.

I didn't, but if I had, I'd have lied. I prayed this was a prelude to something grand.

It was. "I am sampling the sweetbreads in urchin sauce at Ernesto's this Thursday. Would you care to join my party?"

"I adore thymus glands. I would be honored."

Our party was comprised of three well-heeled couples. I was indisputably Ben Hamilton's date. Oh, the unspeakable pleasure of being on a celebrity's arm, even if the arm was attached to a shoulder that barely grazed my bicep. Besides, Ben's effect on the restaurant staff was that of a seven-foot-tall and possibly benevolent god. I knew now what Nancy Kissinger, Sophia Loren, and surely Diane Keaton in her Woody era knew: that short men could be immensely powerful beings, willfully terrorizing master chef to busboy.

The six of us unfolded our napkins as Ben uncapped his pen and ordered the entire meal. Appetizers covered the table. "Let me squeeze just a drop of fresh lime onto your mussel," he said to me, solicitously. And one drop is exactly what he squeezed, rerouting the second one onto the tablecloth. "Just enough to refresh," he explained. I ate it, and he was absolutely correct: two drops would have overwhelmed the poor bivalve, while one drop made it sing.

"Isn't Ben amazing?" a blond woman across the table asked, appraising me more blatantly than Ben did the goat-cheese-and-sweet-onion crêpes. I wondered if I'd taken her rightful place beside the king.

"Yes," I answered, pleasantly. Ben scribbled on his notepad.

Sweetbreads arrived; we discussed their tenderness, the complexity of their sauce. Wine flowed, as did well-pondered pronouncements on the tartness of the raspberries in crème fraîche.

Ben leaned toward me, the slightest trace of crème on his mustache. "Are you having a good time?" he asked.

"I'm in heaven," I told him.

I suppose this was the correct answer, because I was invited to the next five dinners. The membership of the convivial core group rotated, depending on who was in town, who owed whom what favor, who had a special feeling for sashimi. By the third dinner I realized I would never get to make a pithy comment about escargots and Pernod—not because Ben didn't order them, but because only Ben got to make the pithy remarks. By the fourth dinner it occurred to me that Ben was starting to like me in my eggplant dress even better than he liked braised eggplant salad. By the fifth dinner I stopped feeling so intimidated.

"I made a duck in cherry sauce once," I announced to the table. "But I couldn't figure out how to carve it. I think you have to be a surgeon." The less-than-convivial blonde gave me a smug glance. "Well, do *you* know how to carve a duck?" I asked her.

"It's a snap," Ben said. "You just need the right knives. And, of course, the love affair between duck and cherry has long been over."

I knew that, naturally—my duck attempt had been seven years ago—but, ever polite, I did not defend myself. "How would you prepare it?" I asked.

"With juniper berries," he promptly said. Inspiration lit his face. "I'll cook it for you all this Saturday. My house at eight. All right?"

All right? To be personally cooked for by Mr. Benjamin Hamilton? Was this how Priscilla felt when her husband sang "Love Me Tender" a cappella in their bedroom?

I spent one hour and twenty dollars selecting the wine to bring to Ben's duck dinner. At least, I finally figured, if it wasn't appropriate, it also wasn't cheap. When I arrived at Ben's spotless and cleverly decorated apartment, he was holding court in his model kitchen, emperor of the butcher block. We guests sipped champagne from chilled, flute-shaped glasses and exclaimed happily over the first course of angel-hair pasta in a red pepper pureé. As everyone applauded, Ben turned directly to me and said, "What do *you* think?"

I was staring at his perfectly alphabetized spice rack. "It's delicious," I said.

He beamed. A different wine was served with each course, and my wine wasn't one of them. "Let me show you how to carve the duck," he said, leading me to the huge cutting board. He stood behind me, struggling to rest his chin on my shoulder, and guided my hand. "See how easy it is?" he encouraged, squeezing my thickening waist.

I inhaled. "The duck smells like gin."

"That's because gin is made with juniper berries," he said. "Very aromatic. And lovely, like yourself."

I had never been compared to a juniper berry before, but maybe it was harmless enough. On the other hand, maybe it wasn't. The next morning at eleven, my doorbell rang. When I answered it, a delivery boy handed me a large bouquet of gorgeous red radicchio.

The card read: "To my lovely juniper berry. I would have grilled these if I could. Love, Ben."

Now what? Although I felt no guilt about eating dinners he wasn't paying for anyway, this juniper berry business was something else. Was I leading him on?

I put my radicchio in water and pondered a romance with Benjamin Hamilton. If there were a chance for passion, it would have to flower on a turf not entirely his own. How could I get to know the real Ben if he were constantly surrounded with gastronomical sycophants? Could Jerry Hall relate to Mick if they never left the rock concert? Perhaps an all-day hike on Mount Tamalpais would help: no waiters, no convivial guests, just sunshine, green hills, and fresh air.

I decided to invite Ben on such an outing when I called to thank him for the bouquet. He loved the idea, but wondered aloud what food to bring.

"I'll make some sandwiches," I said. "And I'll bring some trail mix."

"*Trail mix?*" he echoed, as if this described the animal leavings one encountered on trails.

"Well, I know it's not wonderful, but it is quick energy."

"Perhaps I could bring a few items."

What would they be, I wondered. Roast quail stuffed with pancetta and fresh sage? Mangoes in cream?

"Fine," I said, cheerily. "I'll see you tomorrow at ten."

I was the picture of the well-adjusted outdoor woman by ten the next morning. But where was Ben? My hiking shoes were on, the ham on rye wrapped and ready to go. It was eleven, then it was twelve. The doorbell rang.

"Sorry," he said. "I had trouble locating the right pâté."

"Pâté?" I said. "In the sun? It'll melt."

He insisted it wouldn't, but it did, all three kinds. All day Ben carried a baguette that was half his height; it turned to cement by the end of our walk.

"I *made* sandwiches," I reminded him, handing him one. He stared at it.

"I used Dijon mustard."

He sniffed slightly. "I'm not an outdoor type," he admitted as we sat down to admire the view. He put his hand on my knee. "Would you like to help me review Robert's Bistro tonight?"

I declined. I told him I'd like him to meet some of my friends, that Dennis and June were giving a barbecue and all we had to do was bring our own meat. Could I help it if all social events are centered around food?

"I would love to meet your friends," he said. "I'll supply our main course."

My love of fine cuisine aside, to me a barbecue is still a barbecue —a good, old-fashioned, all-American tradition whether you use mesquite or not. Though once in a while I'll marinate a chicken, I am usually quite happy with burgers and dogs with sesame-seed buns. But it was not to be: as Dennis and June's grill sizzled with beef patties and foot-long hot dogs, Ben carefully laid our meal alongside: marinated duck liver and rabbit parts brushed with mustard.

Everyone gathered around to look. "Duck liver?" said my friend Bill. Bill is big and likes sweet-pickle relish.

"A delicacy," Ben assured him.

"I didn't even know those little quack-quacks *had* livers," guffawed Bill, grabbing another Rainier Ale.

"It sounds delicious," June said diplomatically.

"It will be," Ben said. When it was ready, Ben made up two perfect plates garnished with the papaya and ginger salad he'd brought himself and insisted we eat at the end of the table, away from the group.

"Don't you want to try June's potato salad?" I asked.

"Certainly not," he said. "This meal cries for papaya." My guilt, as I ate, was twofold: our elitist meal tasted absolutely terrific and I, too, had no craving for June's potato salad. I was also guilty because throughout the repast Ben stared into my eyes and told me I was his juniper berry.

"I don't think I am," I told him.

He looked huffy. "It's because I'm short, isn't it?"

No, it's because you're crazy, a voice inside me said. But instead I told him, "If you really like me, then you should let me do something for *you*. Let's spend a quiet evening together. At *my* house. I'll do all the work this time." I knew that no matter how hard I labored over cookbooks and Cuisinarts I could never come up with a meal that would meet his standards—but, perversely enough, I didn't feel like trying.

Cooking badly is surprisingly easy and takes hardly any time at all. By the time Ben arrived the Cheese Whiz waited in delicate twirls upon the Ritz crackers, assembled on my coffee table alongside the bottle of Thunderbird.

"Ice?" I asked, tossing some cubes into a Fred Flintstone glass I had leftover from childhood.

I could see he didn't know if I was serious, but I kept my countenance sincere.

"You don't seem very hungry," I said, pointing to the untouched hors d'oeuvres. "Wait till you try the salad. You won't resist that." At the table I presented him with a perfect square of lime Jell-O filled with miniature marshmallows and pimento and gaily topped with a dollop of Miracle Whip. "Come on and *eat,*" I said with a straight face. He reached for the Thunderbird instead.

But I would not be put off. "Now for the pièce de résistance," I said. I'd read the recipe for Frito Pie in a women's magazine. You open a giant bag of Frito corn chips, dump in hot canned chili and grated cheese and onion, mix lightly, and serve directly from the bag. I guess the theory is that the chips melt into a pleasantly pliable state.

It was almost painful to observe Ben's face. I thought he might be sick; then I thought he might cry. "Ben, don't you like it? Aren't I your juniper berry?"

He threw down his paper napkin. "You are not!" he squeaked, rising and heading for the door. "You are perfectly disgusting!" he called over his shoulder. "To think I grilled a duck's liver for you!"

Goodbye, Masa's. Goodbye, free meals. I don't even care, and that is the problem. Do you think it's fun to find myself craving Kraft's Macaroni and Cheese in the wee hours? It's Ben's fault that I, a woman once obsessed with every subtle variation of fine cuisine, now eschew Godiva chocolates in favor of M&Ms.

He out-obsessed me.

I wonder if Priscilla Presley lost her taste for rock; I wonder if she listened to opera in the privacy of her room.

Together

9. Dialing Direct

Nicole's telephone problem escaped Paul's notice until the day they moved in together. The telephone, that seemingly innocent hunk of plastic that everyone owned and used, became the subject of their first argument. Nicole wanted a phone with a twenty-five-foot cord and a call-waiting feature. Paul did not.

"Those long cords get tangled up all the time. And you can never *find* the phone when it's ringing. I don't want to break my neck tripping over a twenty-five-foot cord."

"How can I talk on the deck without one?" Nicole implored, green eyes opened wide.

"Why do you have to talk on the deck?"

"I'll be sunbathing there."

"We live in a fog bank."

"It has to get sunny *some*time."

He agreed to the long cord. "But I hate call-waiting," he insisted. "Being put on hold during a personal call is obnoxious."

"I don't want to risk anyone getting a busy signal when they call us," she said.

"I don't get that many calls, so it doesn't matter to me. How many calls do *you* get a day, anyway?" he asked, realizing for the first time that he had no idea what Nicole's phone habits were. He'd heard cohabitation was fraught with danger.

"Not that many," she said vaguely. "I just don't like to miss any of them." She put her arms around his waist. "I'll pay for it. I'll pay for the cord too. And, in exchange, I won't scream about your putting a TV in the bedroom."

"Is this what they call negotiation?" he asked, kissing her. He adored Nicole. If she wanted all her phone calls interrupted, what was the harm? Especially if he could watch sports while lying in bed without feeling guilty.

Cohabitation self-consciousness set in immediately. Nicole no longer gave herself egg-white facials or changed into her bathrobe ten minutes after getting home from work. Paul stopped buying sardines and cut his sports viewing in half. Neither admitted to liking to watch the news during dinner.

Nicole's first marathon call took place one week after they moved in. They were midway through dinner (without watching the news) when the phone rang. Before Paul could differentiate the ring from the scream of the tea kettle, Nicole had flown to the living room and picked up the receiver.

"Hi, Millie," he heard her say. He helped himself to more cassoulet, wondering why he was self-conscious about liking sardines when they were dining on beans and franks. "Anorexic?" he heard Nicole say next. "Is that what the doctor said?" Paul served himself more salad and waited. "Seventy pounds? For real?"

He turned toward the living room. "Your dinner's getting cold," he said. "Why don't you call her back?"

Nicole put her hand over the mouthpiece and said, "I'll be there in a minute."

Paul cleared his plate, then sat down to a cup of herbal tea. He was wondering if he should clear Nicole's plate too when she returned to the table with the phone on her lap. Her left hand held the receiver, her right her fork. Paul marveled at the coordination of speech and ingestion of cassoulet; she never missed a beat.

"I have to go," he said, pointing to his watch. "I'm playing basketball tonight."

Nicole smiled and waved her goodbye as she explained to Millie the perils of bulimia versus anorexia. How could she discuss bulimia while eating? Paul wondered. Nicole had whipped through the rest of the salad and the cassoulet's last white bean without one interruption to her conversational zeal.

" 'Bye!" he said, putting on his jacket as she began to wash the dishes, receiver propped on her shoulder.

"Speak up, Millie, I've got running water," he heard her say as he closed the front door. Three hours later, as he hung up his jacket in the hall closet, he heard her soft voice drifting from the living room. "Paul's home," she was saying. "Talk to you later." Click.

She jumped up to greet him. "How was the game?" she asked.

"Great. We won. Who was on the phone?" He put his arms around her and nuzzled her dark hair.

"Millie."

"No, I mean just now."

"Millie."

"You talked to Millie for three hours?" he said, holding her at arm's length.

She rolled herself back into his arms. "Yeah, so what?"

=

"I guess I'm pretty dumb," Paul told his friend Jack at lunch the next day. "It never even occurred to me she was on the same call the whole evening."

"That's 'cuz you've never lived with a woman before," Jack said, smothering his giant hamburger with ketchup. "They live on the goddamn phone."

"I don't get it. I hate the phone. I only use it when I have to."

"Me too. I always make Carol make dinner reservations and call theaters for show times. The phone makes me nervous." Jack piled tomato and red onion slices on his burger, doubling its size.

"I think it has the opposite effect on Nicole—it calms her down."

"I don't like talking to someone I can't see. Know what I mean?" Jack lifted his burger to his mouth. "Goddamn French rolls. They're too big to eat."

"The phone's unnatural."

"So are women." Jack put down his burger in frustration.

"Cut it in half, goon," Paul said.

Jack seized his uncut burger and forced it into his mouth. "Only women do that," he mumbled, ketchup running down his chin.

═══

Paul noticed that whenever he came home the phone was in use. Nicole talked regularly to Millie, Sharon, and Lisa; they were her single friends. Judy and Diane comprised the second string; they couldn't stay on the phone too long because they lived with men.

"Why don't you all meet for drinks once a week and get it all out at once?" Paul asked.

"You know how busy we are," Nicole said. "It's almost impossible for six women to find an open night together. Besides, I like to talk one on one."

"So two of you can talk about everybody else?" Paul asked.

Nicole glared at him. "We do not engage in idle gossip."

"What do you talk about?"

"Life."

Paul slapped his own face. "Imagine that."

"Sarcasm does not become you," she said, carrying the phone to the bedroom.

"Who are you calling now?" Paul asked, trailing after her.

"My mother, if you don't mind."

"Why should I mind?" He had the sensation of drowning in a whirlpool of high-pitched, girlish voices.

===

"It's Freudian," Jack said to Paul over lunch. It was pseudo-diet day; they were eating chef's salads submerged in bleu cheese dressing.

"What do *you* know about Freud?"

"I know penis envy. Women want their own appendage, so they use the phone."

"Come on," Paul scoffed.

"Think about it. They touch it, they talk to it."

"And that's supposed to be like having a penis?"

Jack punched him in the shoulder, shaking with laughter. "Sure, Paul! Hey—don't you talk to it?"

===

The only good thing about the call-waiting feature, Paul decided, was that he could always get through to Nicole. He called her one evening from work to say he'd be home an hour late.

"No problem," she said sweetly but shortly.

"Go ahead and eat if you're hungry. Don't wait for me."

"Okay."

"Love me?"

"Yes."

"Tell me."

"Paul, dinner's burning on the stove."

"Are you sure you don't have another call on hold?"

"Of course not. Do you think I talk on the phone day and night?"

The telltale click of a holding caller hanging up the phone sounded in both their ears. "What was that?" Paul asked.

"What was what?"

"Nicole, you lied to me. You were talking to someone before I called."

"Just Millie."

"I don't care who it was, I care that you lied. Good relationships are based on trust."

"It's just that you make me so self-conscious about the phone. You force me to lie to you."

"Remember Ray Milland in *Lost Weekend?* Remember all the devious ways he had of hiding his liquor?"

"I've never seen it." The phone clicked again. "Paul, someone's calling. I'll see you when you get home, sweetheart."

=====

Perhaps Nicole had never seen *Lost Weekend* but, Paul noted, she still knew a lot about sneaky behavior. One morning he awoke at 3:00 A.M. alone in bed. He went to the living room and found Nicole nestled in the corner of the sectional couch, a bundle of white terrycloth with a phone attached to her head. "Can't you get him to go to a psychiatrist?" Nicole was whispering into the mouthpiece.

"It's three in the morning," Paul said, naked and cold.

"Diane's husband just flipped out," Nicole whispered to him. "I'll be off as soon as she calms down." She returned to the phone.

Paul stood there, thinking about how he hadn't, in the one month they'd lived there, stood naked in the living room at 3:00 A.M. before. It was an unexpectedly sexy time and place. He wanted to make love to her right there at the apex of the sectional couch.

"Nicole," he said, stepping toward her, reaching for the sash of her robe.

"I'm on the phone!" she hissed.

Paul stopped in his tracks. Maybe Jack was right. The phone receiver was obviously the most popular appendage in the house.

=====

"I feel sexually rejected," Paul confided to Jack over their next lunch.

"Who doesn't?" Jack said, disdainfully removing the anchovies from his side of the pizza.

"It's the phone. She's on it all the time. Last night I followed the phone cord and caught her talking inside the hall closet with the door closed."

"Pretty weird."

"It reminds me of my brother Ronnie when he was coked out. My whole family had to go to Al-Anon meetings. You know, to cope with his lying and everything." Paul put Jack's discarded anchovies on his half of the pizza. "Did you ever see *Lost Weekend?*"

"No."

"Never mind. I wonder if there's Phone-Anon."

═

There wasn't, Paul discovered, after looking in the directory. He tried to talk to Nicole in a nonthreatening way. "Speaking purely for myself," he said jovially over Sunday breakfast, "phone conversations are unsatisfying. I need to see the person's face, read the expressions."

Nicole was jovial too. "I'm completely the opposite. I visualize the person while I'm talking. In fact, later on I can't even remember if the conversation took place in person or on the phone. Isn't that something?"

"Speaking purely for myself," Paul tried again, "I'd prefer to go to someone's house and converse directly every two weeks rather than settle for a phone conversation once a day."

"I'm completely the opposite. I don't consider a phone conversation second best. If it's a rainy night and neither party feels like getting in the car and driving somewhere, why not have the visit on the phone? It's just as good."

"The phone is some invention, isn't it?" he said.

═

His brother Ronnie had recovered fully from his addiction, and Paul was certain that Nicole could, too. She needed love and understanding and maybe a little aversion therapy.

"Is this supposed to be funny?" Nicole asked him one night, pointing to the perforated sandpaper glued to the receiver.

"There's nothing funny about this," Paul said.

"I'll say. You could have injured my ear."

Paul was surprised her ears weren't injured already. How did they hold up to this constant abuse? Years of training, he supposed. She'd probably gotten hooked on a Princess telephone when she was sixteen and then graduated to the heavier stuff: push buttons, extensions, conference calls.

"What's this awful smell?" Nicole asked the next day, pushing the phone's mouthpiece under Paul's nose.

"Bitters."

"Like you put in cocktails?"

"My Aunt Lily put bitters on her breasts when she wanted to wean little Stevie."

"That's disgusting."

"It worked."

"I am not a baby, Paul."

"You're my baby," he said, embracing her. "I love you, Nicole. I want to help you."

"I love you, too, but I don't need any help."

Denial, he knew, was the biggest obstacle. How could he help her when she wouldn't acknowledge that she had a problem? He kissed her tenderly. She kissed him back. Then the phone rang and she scampered away.

=====

"Okay, forget Freud," Jack told Paul over after-work drinks. "It's obvious Nicole is afraid of getting close. You're her first serious relationship and she can't stand the pressure. So she's put the phone right smack between you."

"I thought men were supposed to be afraid of intimacy, not women."

"Men always get a bad rap. Everything's supposed to be our fault. But women are weird, man."

"So what should I do?"

"Show her the real you. Be vulnerable. Let her know that she can do the same."

Paul pondered what the real him might be. Probably someone who loved sardines, watched twice as much sports, and liked to watch the news during dinner. If he revealed these things to Nicole, would she feel secure enough to respond in kind?

She might, he thought, if he revealed them on the phone.

"Thanks," Paul said, dropping a five-dollar-bill on the bar and dashing out the door.

═══

Nicole came home from work, resisted putting on her bathrobe, and sat on the couch with the day's mail. The phone rang.

"Oh hi, Paul. You working late?"

"No, I just wanted to hear your voice. How are you?"

"Okay. I was just going to fix dinner. Have a yen for anything special?"

"Canned sardines on pumpernickel with hot mustard."

Nicole grimaced. "Are you serious? I hate sardines."

"Everyone does except me and my brother Ronnie. I just thought it was time you knew that about me."

Nicole laughed. "Okay, now your deep, dark secret is out. Any others?"

"I wanted a TV in the bedroom because my favorite thing in the world, next to making love to you, is watching sports while lying in bed drinking a beer."

"But you've never done that."

"I didn't want you to think I was a slob."

"I wouldn't."

"But I was afraid you would. Now I have to tell you something else. Ready?"

"I think so." It was strange talking to Paul on the phone for so long.

"When I lived alone I always watched the news during dinner."

Nicole gulped. "Paul, so did I."

"Still love me?"

"Paul, I miss you. Come home."

"I am home."

"What?"

"I'm calling you from the bedroom. Come see."

Nicole carried her phone down the hall, opened the bedroom door, and saw Paul lying on their bed talking into a brand new push-button phone.

"I had it installed this afternoon while you were at work," he said, still speaking into the receiver. She could hear him in stereo.

Nicole realized that she'd never, in the two months they'd lived there, stood in the hall at 6:00 P.M. and watched Paul talk on the phone while lying on their double bed. It was a surprisingly sexy time and place.

"You look very enticing lying there," she said into her phone.

"Want to join me?" he said into his. The stereophonic effect was somehow pleasing.

"Yes." She started toward him.

"Well, you can't. I want to keep talking. I want you to go back to the living room and keep talking to me. And if you hear a 'call-waiting' click, I don't want you to answer it. Just talk to me."

"Really?"

"Really."

Nicole retreated to the living room. "What shall we talk about?" she asked.

"Us. Starting with you. Do you have any deep, dark secrets?"

She huddled into the apex of the sectional couch. "Well, I used to smear egg whites on my face to tighten my pores."

"I bet you looked beautiful."

"No, it's horrible."

"Anything else?"

Nicole closed her eyes. "Okay. When I lived alone, I changed into my bathrobe every night as soon as I got home."

"You look gorgeous in your robe."

"No, I don't."

"I admit you look even better without it." She was hearing him in stereo again. She opened her eyes to see Paul reaching for the zipper of her dress. "Let me help you out of this," he said, still into the phone.

"I see you got a twenty-five-foot cord, too." She started to hang up.

"No, keep talking," he insisted. He fell upon her in a fifty-foot mess of tangled phone cord. They both forgot about dinner.

===

Jack was tackling another giant hamburger and keeping his distance from Paul's sardine sandwich. "So have things improved?" he asked. "Does Nicole like your having your own line?"

Paul grinned. Nicole had cut out all phone calls except to her mother and to Diane, whose husband was still flipping out. She now talked to Millie, Sharon, Lisa, and Judy at lunch during weekdays. Lunch was a great institution, Paul thought. You could solve a lot of problems over lunch.

"Yeah, she thinks it's great. She even calls me sometimes."

"You mean from home?"

"Yeah. She likes to call me from the living room while I'm in the bedroom."

"Huh?"

"Well, let's just say we've never been closer."

"Congratulations. I'm glad to hear it."

Paul bit hungrily into his sandwich. Communication was wonderful. He adored Nicole. He thought he might call her as soon as they both got home and ask her to marry him.

10. Confession, Truth and Lies

One afternoon during our eighteenth summer, I was shopping with my best friend, Louise. A woman in her forties stopped us on the street. "Louise!" she said, "I haven't seen you in years. How nice to run into you like this. How is your mother?"

She's fine, Mrs. Anderson, thank you," Louise said calmly, while my mouth fell open. Louise's mother had been dead for two years. "Lovely to see you again," she added, moving quickly on to the next store.

With Mrs. Anderson out of earshot, I confronted my friend. "I can't believe you lied," I told her. "She'll feel terrible when she finds out the truth. And she'll think you're crazy."

I saw tears in Louise's eyes. "I don't care how Mrs. Anderson feels. I'm not going to stand on the street talking about my mother's death with anybody. Not with anybody, understand?"

My mother is alive and well and I did not actually understand at all. At eighteen, I did not yet know a loss so severe that I could not bear to articulate it. Nor did I know that silence and ambiguity were available options for evading the truth. I believed in telling the truth, and, like most of my female friends, I also believed heartily in confession: not only must the truth be told, but it had to be told to everybody, and right away.

I know that the confessional aspect of the female personality drives men insane. The only thing that baffles them more is the female penchant for going to the bathroom in groups, and even this is a variation on the confessional theme—the need to make experience collective.

"Why does all of California have to know about our sex life?" my college boyfriend asked me.

"Because they have to know about mine, and you're the one I'm having it with."

"Is nothing sacred?"

I thought a minute. "No," I decided, with sophomoric zeal.

I lived with four female roommates all through college. Fueled by verbiage, we continually revealed, discussed, and rehashed the details of our lives. Ultimately, an event entered the sphere of reality for us only when it was verbalized.

I remember receiving a frenzied phone call from my friend Sharon early one Sunday morning. "I just spent the night with the hottest man in San Francisco. I think I'm in love! Can you meet me for brunch?"

"Aren't you having breakfast with him?"

"I sent him home already."

"You sent the hottest man in San Francisco home by nine-thirty on a Sunday morning?"

Sharon almost squealed with impatience. "Well, what's the point of falling in love if I can't tell you about it?"

My girlfriends and I believed fervently that the unexamined life was not worth living. And, logically, this axiom rendered the lives of our boyfriends and brothers virtually worthless.

"What do you say about me to your friends?" I asked my college boyfriend in that inane, narcissistic manner of young lovers. Tell me how cute and clever I am, was my silent command.

"I don't talk about you."

"You *what*?"

"I don't really talk to anyone else. You're my only friend."

Every girl I knew was told by her boyfriend that she was, in fact, his one and only confidante.

"It's weird to be Bill's only conduit to reality," my roommate Gail mused. "What did guys do before sex? Maintain eighteen years of mute solitude?"

"Yes," the circle of roommates responded in a chorus.

"No wonder guys peak sexually at eighteen. It's not sex at all —it's human communication. It's the first time they ever talked to anybody!"

"What do they do between girlfriends?" I asked. "Resume the vows of silence?"

"Yes," said Gail. "That's probably why they always find a new one so fast. You can live without sex longer than you can live without conversation, once you've been introduced to it."

"I'd rather never speak again than go without sex," breathed Sharon, still allied with the hottest man in San Francisco.

If women are more confessional than men, it does not necessarily follow that they are more truthful. Confession invites elaboration, a playful rearrangement of facts to heighten entertainment value.

Louise told a twenty-minute anecdote at a dinner party once; only her boyfriend and I, having heard the story in its evolutionary stages, knew that its final polished version was largely fictitious. I didn't mind this, because the essence of the story was intact, its purpose fulfilled.

But her boyfriend was furious. "You *lied*, Louise," he accused her after dinner.

"Don't be so literal," she retorted. "It's a story!"

"But all those people thought it was true."

"It doesn't *matter*," she insisted, trying to make him see what he truly could not see.

If women and men both lie, I'm sure women do a better job of it if only because they are generally more creative with spoken language.

"A man lies by omission," Louise explained to me once. "He forgets to mention that he's sleeping with your best friend. Then when you find out, he insists he never lied about it; he'd have given you an honest answer if you'd asked him a direct question."

I knew a man once who was a relentless truth-teller. Just graduated from law school, he told me his love of truth was a highly held principle. I believed him until the evening he cooked dinner for me, finishing off the meal with a romantic cognac in front of the fire. He stared into said fire, without speaking, for thirty minutes. I know because I looked at my watch.

"What are you thinking about?" I finally asked him, gently. It had been a half hour; I was curious.

"None of your business," he replied.

Oh. I sat for another five minutes, wondering if you could permanently blind someone with cognac, and said, "Mark, if you don't want me to know what you're thinking about, just make something up. Say you're thinking about world peace."

He told me a week later that our mutual friend Barbara was better looking than I was. "I know she is," I said. "Barbara is better looking than *anybody*, but you've just broken a major rule of sexual etiquette."

"What's sexual etiquette?" he asked. I realized then that Mark knew little of either sex or manners, let alone their essential combination.

"You're supposed to pretend that the person you're sleeping with is better looking than anyone in the room. Or the world."

"Oh yeah?"

"Sure. I do with you."

Mark used the truth to vent his considerable hostility; I continued to tell the truth largely because I didn't think I could get away with lying. Louise, after two years in social work, came to me with this revelation: "Honesty is an American obsession, just like punctuality. But it's all open to interpretation. In other cultures, people tell you what they think you want to hear. They want you to feel happy. If that requires a lie, they regard it as the morally correct choice."

I spent three years with a man who was raised in Central America. He explained Latin time to me: "If we say we'll be there at two on Thursday, it just means that we'll be there on Thursday. Sometimes Friday."

It was hard to adjust to this jetlagged sense of time, but I did begin to see the wisdom in telling him what, as Louise put it, I thought he wanted to hear.

"Did you buy this wine at that shop on Twenty-fourth Street?" he'd ask me.

"Do you want it to be from that shop on Twenty-fourth Street?"

"Well, it's a good place to buy wine. They know what they're doing."

I'd bought it at Safeway but I didn't want to get in trouble. "I got it at that shop on Twenty-fourth Street," I assured him. He was appeased; I was spared the lecture on bourgeois consumerism.

A lie about the wine shop was acceptable to me, but I could not condone the larger deceptions. When Gail's parents were in town, we met them for lunch. Gail's father invited us to rejoin them at their hotel at five for drinks, after we had run our respective Saturday errands.

"We'll see you in the lobby at five," my boyfriend assured them charmingly, shaking their hands all around. I knew this was a lie; he had something else planned.

"Why did you say that?" I asked in the car.

"It's easier."

"But they'll expect us."

"No, they won't."

"Yes, they *will*. They're Anglos. God, how embarrassing." As much as Mark used truth as a vehicle for brutality, I suspect my boyfriend did the same with his definition of the permissible lie. Though he attributed it to cultural training, I saw later that his behavior was selective. When his own family was involved, he was never even five minutes late.

I was decimated when we broke up, so decimated that for the first time in my life I did not want to talk about it. Confession would exacerbate, not ease, this pain. Fifteen years after the fact I finally understood Louise's stance with Mrs. Anderson. Silence was an option, and more easily exercised than I ever imagined.

I was surprised to learn two things: people have no choice but to respect your right to silence, and, it drives them absolutely nuts.

"Do you want to talk about it?" Debbie asked me gently, as she drove us to the new Thai restaurant.

"No," I answered pleasantly.

Her disappointment was palpable. "Perhaps later on," she urged softly, trying to sound understanding. People speak softly when they want you to think they understand you.

"No, actually, I'm never going to talk about it," I informed her. "How's the curry at this place, anyway?"

It is sad but undeniable that luxuriating in the recitation of someone else's tragedy can make a great evening. I knew Debbie had anticipated just such a session, and I had ruined it for her. She'd wanted her marriage confirmed by my separation, her sense of security strengthened by my contrasting disorientation, and plus she just plain wanted the dirt. None of this negated her sympathy for me, which I knew to be heartfelt. She merely needed to hear my confession.

Sometimes verbalization diffuses an experience; other times it clarifies and enhances it. The need for self-containment vies with the need for affirmation. I have finally learned the trick of keeping a secret: you simply do not tell it to anybody and after a while the secret burns away.

"It's not so much the unexamined life that's worthless," Louise told me once, "it's the unshared life. I feel better when I share my stories with people and they recognize them as stories of their own."

My women friends and I still talk too much; we still instinctively grab the phone when there is something to report. We will doubtlessly continue this practice throughout our lives: like confession, it is comforting, and like the truth, it is inevitable.

But now that we're in our thirties we no longer call each other at 9:30 A.M. with sexual revelations; we're too dignified for that. We wait at least until noon.

11. Cheap Men

Judith and Gwen are seated across from one another at a corner table at the Balboa Café. They have each ordered the veal chop special for lunch, and are first sharing a mixed green salad adorned with blue cheese. They are, they both agree, "burgered out." Two glasses of Chardonnay stand half empty before them. On second glance, they may be half full.

"So how is Phil?" Gwen asks Judith.

Judith stops buttering her sourdough bread for a moment. "Cheap," she decides, and picks up her knife once again.

"Cheap? What a shame. I hate cheap men," says Gwen. "How cheap is he?"

"Have you ever heard a buck scream?"

"Sure. Greg can make a buck not only scream, but sob." Greg is the new architect in Gwen's life. She always dates architects because she feels they are artistic without starving in the proverbial garret. She is fond of art.

Judith has been dating Phil for a month. He is an attorney. Judith always dates attorneys because they seem to her to have wonderfully ordered minds. She particularly likes litigators, because they are Thespian without starving in that same proverbial garret. "I first realized Phil was cheap when I noticed all the red food we were eating," she muses.

"Oh, the Red Food Syndrome," Gwen laments. "Pizzas, enchiladas. That's cheap, all right." She studies her non-red veal chop. It costs $13.50. "Greg takes me out for red food, too."

A competitive gleam appears in Judith's blue eyes. "Really? And is Greg an aficionado of House Wineries?"

"House Wineries?" Gwen is confused. She toys with a lock of blond hair. "Is that in Napa?"

"Phil thinks so. They make two types of wine: House Red and House White. It's all he'll drink."

Gwen tosses back her non-house wine, laughs, and signals for another round. "Greg's favorite cocktail is wine-with-dinner."

"Phil likes that, too."

"Greg always orders a half carafe. He thinks wine is carafed, not bottled. But he always ends up ordering a second half carafe, which upsets him terribly. Two halves cost more than one whole. But he never has the foresight to order the whole to begin with."

In her zeal, Judith almost forgets her veal chop. "What about driving?" she presses. "Does Greg try to make you drive all the time?"

"Cheap men always try to make you drive," Gwen answers. "They say they're tired but they just don't want to pay for the gas."

"When Phil does drive, the first activity on our Date Agenda is a visit to the gas station. But he never fills the tank. He buys five dollars worth of gas. I think that's about half a cup."

"Greg and I were parked in a gas station last week when he noticed that gas across the street cost four cents less a gallon. He almost smashed into a Mack truck getting over there."

Judith will not be outdone. "When Phil buys his five dollars worth of gas, he has to borrow the money from me. He never has any cash on his person."

Gwen, like Judith, is a professional woman, and can rise to almost any challenge. "Greg," she intones, "banks at Obscurity National. They have one automatic teller and no one has found it yet. I mean, this man *never* has cash."

"When we go to North Beach on a Saturday night," offers Judith with equal solemnity, "Phil refuses to park in a lot. He drives around for two hours waiting for Godot to pull out of that perfect spot in front of Emilio's."

"Greg won't park in a lot unless I cry and take Valium out of my purse."

"Phil has never bought a round in his life."

"Greg thinks a round is a song."

The waiter clears their plates and Judith and Gwen lean back in their chairs, exhausted. They order cappuccinos for a caffeine rush. They do not, of course, order a fattening dessert.

"When I used to date photographers and painters," Gwen remembers, "I didn't mind eating red food with them. In fact, I paid for both our meals a good deal of the time."

"But those men were poor, not cheap," Judith reminds her. "Poor artists can get away with it. Until they're about thirty-five, anyway."

"If Greg were poor, his cheapness would be tolerable. But he talks all through dinner about his forty-dollar haircut that didn't work out and then stiffs the waiter on his tip. He doesn't notice the discrepancy."

"Cheap men don't notice much of anything. If they did, they'd know how damaging cheapness is to their masculinity and start buying drinks for everyone in the world."

"Judith, you're a sexist."

"Okay, I'm sexist but I'm also right. Some character flaws are more offensive in one gender than the other. It's a cultural truth. A drunk, profane woman always seems worse than a drunk, profane man. Her femininity is undercut. And a cheap man is unmanly. It's insidious. It's like a man who gets fat—he doesn't merely get fat, he develops breasts and becomes womanly. But not in a good way." Judith orders another cappuccino.

"Your logic astounds me. I think you've been dating attorneys for too long," says Gwen. "Explain yourself. If cheap men seem womanly, does that mean that women are cheap?"

"No. They've always had that reputation, but it's only because they've always been poor. Why should someone who earns fifty-nine cents to the male dollar throw her money around?"

"Good point. Except I happen to know that you earn as much as Phil," Gwen emphasizes. "Since your promotion anyway."

Judith leans forward for an intimate moment. "Gwen, I'll tell you something. Deep in my heart I haven't given up the dream of having a provider. I mean, I'm intellectually reconciled to supporting myself forever, but I was nonetheless brought up in a world where women worked at home and men paid the bills. It still has a mystique to me. When a man buys me dinner, I feel as if some ancient cosmic order has been reconfirmed."

Gwen leans forward, too. "You're crazy," she whispers.

Judith smiles, unoffended, and looks over the check. "You owe twenty-eight fifty," she says. "With tax and tip."

"Let me see that." Gwen takes the check from Judith's grasp. "You had two cappuccinos. You owe three dollars more."

"But you insisted on blue cheese on the salad. I don't even like blue cheese. So you should pick up that extra seventy-five cents."

"Actually, you still owe me for lunch that day when you couldn't find your Visa card. If you pay for this, we'll be about even."

"I don't think so. Wait a minute," Judith says, rummaging through her purse. "Let me find my calculator."

"Take your time," says Gwen. She relaxes in her chair, lights a cigarette, and gives the waiter a long, slow wink. She assures him with this gesture that they will pay their bill in due time; he has only to be patient. She assures him that he will most certainly receive a good, even generous, tip.

12. Dangerous Gifts

The best gift I ever received from a man came on my nine-teenth birthday. Artie said he had nothing planned until the evening, when he'd try to scrape up enough money to take me out to dinner. Meanwhile, he had to run an errand for Dennis, his roommate, and would I come along? Dennis had given him an address to find on Market Street, and Artie wasn't sure just where it was. I was not exactly busy, so I joined Artie in the trip across town. We parked his semidevastated sports car in a public garage and ambled down Market Street, he checking the street numbers, I shuffling dejectedly through the discarded trash on the sidewalk, to which I felt akin.

"Is this eleven ninety-two Market Street?" he asked me. We stood in front of the Orpheum Theater where the musical *Hair* was playing. Live! Theater! *Gimmee a head with hair, long, beauti-ful hair!* Why had Dennis sent us here?

"We have *tickets*," Artie explained, nudging me through the entrance. The crushed paper cups in the gutter and I no longer had anything in common. "Happy birthday!" he said, hugging me.

I was speechless with pleasure (*Hair* was *the* cultural event of 1969) and then with despair. "My glasses are in your glove compartment," I blurted. "I won't be able to see anything!" Artie, a nineteen-year-old track star, ran eight blocks to the garage and back before "The Age of Aquarius" was in full swing. If he minded this last-minute dash, he never let me know it, and this is mostly why the gift was so exquisite.

It's been downhill ever since, which makes me sound uncomfortably like Princess Phyllis, a friend who says every September when her birthday rolls around: "If I have to tell Stan what I want, then it's just not the same." Stan gives her the "wrong thing" every year, but Phyllis never tells him what the "right thing" is.

"Is Stan supposed to intuit your secret desire and then make sure it's flawlessly fulfilled?" I ask her. She never responds, so I know the answer is "yes." I also know that Stan will never give her the right thing because it does not exist, at least not in the form of a wrappable gift. Princess Phyllis maintains that royal habit of looking for ways to feel hurt, and she is never (or perhaps she is always, and blissfully), disappointed.

Since the days of Artie I've received gifts from men that were selected not only without intuition, but without a hint of the most rudimentary observation. To wit: a wool (to which I was emphatically allergic) sweater which fit him perfectly. I held this huge, scratchy garment up to my body, struggling to fight off a Princess Phyllis attack. "Have you ever looked at my upper body?" I asked him. It seemed to me a viable question. "It is distinctly medium sized."

I then held the sweater up to his body. "Your size exactly," I assessed, and it was. His face fell, not into chagrin, but into honest perplexity. He had no idea how he had selected such a gift. The ramifications (a narcissism so consuming that he only knew his own body type?) were too upsetting to contemplate, so I asked him only two things: "Does this remind you of seventh grade, when you gave your mother a Beach Boys album?" and "Did you keep the sales slip?"

As long as a man keeps the sales slips, I feel I have no right to complain. Indeed, any right I have to complain is further forfeited by the fact that I am, myself, an inadequate gift-giver. I have little imagination; I cannot envision what it is that men want, other than a good time and a modicum of peace. But what happiness from a department store? I usually buy a bottle of good Scotch (albeit not for sworn bourbon drinkers) or cook a zanier meal than usual and call it Birthday Dinner. I've never run across the male counterpart of Princess Phyllis, thank God; I think, in general, men are happy to receive any gift at all.

My close friend Alan recalls gifts from his ex-wife with fond nostalgia. "Remember what a great cook Corinne was?" he often asks me, usually after we've shared a mediocre meal downtown. To ease his pain, he refers to Corinne as if she were either dead or no longer cooking. She is neither.

"Who could forget?" I said. "The worst part of your separation was knowing I'd never again be invited to her dinner parties." Corinne is one of those fearless cooks who can make veal Prince Orloff, Vietnamese shrimp balls and couscous in the same week without flinching.

"When I worked for the welfare department and she wasn't working at all, I came home every day for lunch. I'd be starving. Some days she'd surprise me by opening the door naked, pulling off my clothes, and dragging me to bed. I'd forget all about lunch until I realized we were enveloped in a wonderfully heady nonsexual scent. Corinne would then open the nightstand drawer and bring out my hot lunch."

"Did she do that every day?"

"Oh, no. It was a special present she gave me when she happened to be in the mood. Talk about flair—I'll never be that lucky again. She even put homemade sauerkraut on her Reuben sandwiches."

═══

The inherent politics of buying a man a gift never hit me more strongly than when I was twenty-five and Christmas shopping for the proverbial Rich and Older Man. He was twenty years my senior, and I wanted a present that would reflect my sophistication as well as my ultimate indifference to his affection. "See how thoughtful this young woman is," my gift was to shout, "and yet see how she probably spent no more than ten minutes selecting it! See how busy she is with other preoccupations!"

This was a tall order and one I could not fill myself, so I consulted my friend Roberta, an intuitive, observant woman with classic taste. We spent three hours downtown agonizing in men's clothing shops before settling on a cashmere scarf. This was a chilly December; he might even wear it. It was a small gift but one of high quality. It was blue to match his dimming eyes and better yet, he could wear it, as he did his wardrobe of turtleneck sweaters, to cover his increasingly crepey neck.

He liked it. He liked it so much he reciprocated then and there by opening a living-room cabinet and extracting a tiny bottle of Joy perfume for me. It was one of many stacked there in reserve for such emergency occasions. He probably went through the whole supply that holiday season, a not inexpensive feat.

"At least sign the card," I suggested, indicating the blank tag that dangled from the black bottle. I wanted a souvenir. He signed; we drank sherry. I decided I'd never agonize over a gift again, or at least not for the Older Man, for whom all I ever needed was to be twenty-five. I decided, too, to go ahead and wear jeans the next time I saw him, no matter how much I feared they trivialized me. After all, he wore them often enough.

Gifts are dangerous, because they embody the hidden expectations of the giver and reveal the expectations of the recipient. "It cost under thirty dollars, you don't love me enough," is a silent refrain. They say it's the thought that counts, and for some that's absolutely true. My friend Linda came into a hefty trust fund at age twenty-one, and although the money was more than welcome, it never turned her into Princess Phyllis.

"I used to think the best thing about having money was being able to give my boyfriend expensive presents," she said. "It was exhilarating to buy him something terrific and see how happy it made him. I don't care what anyone says, material things *can* make you happy."

"Of course they can. Do you still buy him expensive gifts?"

"No, I stopped when I realized two things. The first was that I always, no matter how hard I tried not to, managed to let him know exactly what the gift cost. Sometimes I left the price tag on, other times I let him overhear it in a conversation with someone else. But I could see I was trying to get mileage out of it."

"What was the second thing?"

Linda laughed. "Lack of reciprocity! He reasoned that I was rich enough to buy gifts for myself, so he never even bothered to give me a single rose for my birthday. But it was my own fault— I turned it into a competition that only I could win. Or lose, I should say."

Remembering this confession, I made a point of giving Linda a giant heartshaped lollipop for Valentine's Day. She told me later that this gesture had brought her close to tears. She gave up both her boyfriend and her extravagant gifts and eventually married a man who knew the value of a single rose as well as a pair of diamond earrings.

Robbie Anderson and I won the prize for Most Crossed Expectations in Gift Exchange last Christmas. We had enjoyed a summer vacation fling six months before, and were briefly reunited for the holiday season. I think we both expected a relaunching of the Love Boat, but it was apparent to me that the boat was sinking fast as soon as I saw that Robbie hadn't cleaned his apartment once in the decade he'd lived in it. Still, I liked him a lot and was well practiced in pretending I didn't notice intolerable things. And then we opened our presents.

Lacking Linda's trust fund, I had bought him a paperback copy of Robertson Davies's *The Deptford Trilogy,* which is what I give to everybody who I think would prefer it to Scotch. It's the best thing I've ever read; therefore, I want everyone I know to read it. He thanked me and promised to read it right away. I opened my package to find a purple teddy. I, a fan of terrycloth bathrobes and Fruit of the Loom, was dumbfounded. Was this a sex enhancement? Was there any sex to enhance? I didn't know what should happen next: should Robbie give a public reading and I an extemporaneous floor show? He wanted me to try it on immediately. I shuffled tissue paper on top of it and declared I couldn't find it. So there we were: a thwarted sex kitten and a man with a reading assignment. We were not only off the Love Boat; we were swimming in different oceans.

My American Heritage dictionary defines "gift" as "something that is bestowed voluntarily and without compensation." It sounds easy, apolitical. But in reality, a gift is usually bestowed when dictated by the calendar, likening it to chronological blackmail. And no compensation? My cashmere scarf was meant to win approval; Robbie's purple teddy (I left it in his apartment; I pray he's using it as a dustrag) begged for fulfillment of some sexual fantasy. We all should have saved our hard-earned pennies.

I don't think Princess Phyllis is right when she says she shouldn't have to tell Stan what she wants for her birthday. Of course she should tell him. Unfortunately, I don't know how he can possibly give her what I'm sure she craves: a nineteen-year-old track star named Artie racing back for her glasses so she won't miss one visual detail of *Hair*. Poor, hapless Stan. How can he hope to match a standard like that?

13. Professional Couple

When Alex finally invited Sophie to move into his house with him, an interesting thing happened to his name. It became, in Sophie's dulcet tones, elongated, formalized. For the first time in the four years she'd been waiting for him to leave his wife, he became Alexander.

"Alexander and I would like to invite you and Benny over for dinner," she told me on the phone.

At first I didn't know who she meant. "Who?"

"Alexander and I," she repeated, still dulcet.

Benny told me it was one of the first signs. Of what? I wanted to know.

"Of trying to be a professional couple." He had his earphones on, as usual, and was swaying to Mozart as he spoke.

I didn't know what that was. "Are we a professional couple?" I asked.

He shook his head. "Nah—if we were, we'd both be listening to this music."

"Except I can't bear sound before noon," I reminded him.

"I know. But if we were a professional couple, you'd be listening at nine A.M. anyway."

I considered telling Sophie that *Benito* and I would be delighted to come to dinner, but I resisted the temptation and simply told her Benny and I would be there at seven. Why tease Sophie merely because she was slightly delirious from the joy of requited love? She deserved to be happy; she'd fought four long years for this union.

Alex looked much as I remembered him—fair-haired, slight, innocuously pleasant. Sophie, however, was changed. Her eyes were not only glazed over but constantly fastened to Alex's face. It was sort of sweet, I thought. Strange, but sweet.

"We've got Brie and crackers," she informed us, "and Alexander can get your drinks if you know what you'd like." She seemed grateful to be a part of this domestic division of labor at last.

Again, I felt the urge to tease. Can Alexander the Great come up with a steam beer? I wanted to ask. "A beer, please," is what I said. Benny asked for red wine. Our drink orders always confuse waiters, who believe instinctively that beer was created for men and wine for their dates. Alex, seemingly oblivious to his name change, served the drinks. His eyes might be a little glazed over too, I mused, peering at him over my beer.

Perhaps further insight could be gained in the kitchen with the happy hostess. "Can I help?" I asked Sophie.

"Sure," she said. "Let's make the salad." She was serving avocado halves stuffed with shrimp. Holding the two avocados, she muttered, "Damn. Only one of them is ripe. The other one feels like cement."

"So give the guys the cement halves," I tossed off, hardly thinking. "Big deal." I was squeezing lemon juice on the shrimp and searching for dillweed.

"Oh, no," protested Sophie, looking at me as if I'd suggested injecting the cement avocado with cyanide. "Alexander and I will take the hard one. You and Benny are our guests."

I was staggered. All our lives Sophie had been the kind of

woman who believed it was Lucy and Ethel against Fred and Ricky. Why this sudden deference to the Mertzes?

"She who makes the salad should get the ripe avocado," I chanted, as Sophie sliced and peeled. She gave me a vacant look and kept on working.

What a simp, I thought, spooning shrimp into the avocados in what I hoped was an even distribution. And then I was seized by a horrid thought: Maybe I didn't really love Benny. If I truly loved him, I'd never have suggested giving him the cement avocado. Maybe I didn't deserve him, or any man. If I could not make a tiny sacrifice for the man in my life, maybe I was not a Real Woman. Would Benny leave me? I wondered. I'd better straighten up and listen to Mozart in the morning. I hastily spooned extra shrimp onto Benny's salad.

The next week I called Sophie to ask if she wanted to see *Betrayal* with me at a bargain matinee. We had a long history of daytime movies together.

"Alexander doesn't want to see *Betrayal*," she replied.

"Of course he doesn't. No male does. I didn't ask Alex-uh-ander. I asked *you.*"

"Alexander wants to see that new film at the Regency."

I kept staring at the receiver. Was I crazy? This conversation reminded me of the time I had a can of anchovies that required a tricky hand opener I didn't possess. I'd gone next door and asked my neighbor, a hippie who listened to The Grateful Dead quite a bit, if he would mind opening it for me. "I don't like anchovies," he said quietly, after a full minute of staring silently at the can.

═══

"I'll give your regards to Pinter," I promised, hanging up. Benny was on the couch, plugged into Mozart. "Sophie won't go to the movie with me," I complained to him, removing one of his earphones.

"It's probably separation anxiety," he diagnosed. "She doesn't want to leave Alexander the Great."

I asked Benny to come with me instead. He refused.

"Why don't you have separation anxiety about me?" I asked, feeling suddenly deficient again. If I'd insisted on Benny getting the ripe avocado, he'd probably see *Betrayal* with me. I guess we just don't love each other enough, I thought, walking alone to the bus stop.

Two weeks later brought my birthday and Benny made me one of his incredible Italian sausage omelets. He served it to me in bed, an annual tradition, and brought in the mail. "Look, five cards," he reported. "Not bad. See how popular you are?"

One was from my dentist, one from an insurance company, and one, it seemed from the handwriting, from Sophie. Correction. Upon opening the card, I saw it was from Sophie *and* Alex-ANDER.

"I can't stand this," I moaned, pushing the remaining half of my omelet aside.

"What?"

"I can't stand women who send cards and sign their boyfriend's name to it. Alex doesn't know it's my birthday and if he did know he wouldn't care. Why can't she just sign her own name?"

"I explained this to you already. She's trying to establish a Professional Couple."

"Remind me never to sign your name to a card," I said. Not much chance of that. Benny and I sent out different sets of Christmas cards every year. I liked contemporary, irreverent cards, and he preferred what I call Sentimental Schlock. Our mutual friends received one of each. Was this wrong? Should I just sign my name to the schlocky cards? Maybe I was not standing by my man. Would Tammy Wynette tell me I was making a big mistake? And wasn't she married four times?

I wasn't going to let this ruin my birthday, so Benny and I went to see *Betrayal* (I had to see it a second time, and he agreed to accompany me "but only as a birthday gesture") and invited Sophie and Alex over for a birthday dinner.

"You know, I accidentally liked that movie," Benny admitted to me when we stopped to buy the dinner groceries.

"See what joys togetherness can bring?" I said, feeling unexpected anxiety.

We spent the evening watching Sophie sit, in distinctly canine fashion, at Alex's feet. She stared at him with that beatific glaze that fascinated me so. It intrigued me and it annoyed me; in any case, I was beginning to feel hypnotized by her hypnotic state. Alex returned her gaze every fifteen minutes or so, mostly when she handed him a drink, a smoked oyster, or a clean ashtray. When he got up to use the bathroom, I was tempted to say, "Hadn't you better follow him?" I didn't say it, and I didn't need to. She did follow him.

"Benny, why is she in the bathroom with him?" I asked helplessly.

"Sex or drugs, I guess," he said. "Or just more separation anxiety."

I remembered when I was eighteen a celebrated college couple I knew insisted on drinking coffee from the same mug, passing it back and forth between them in the supreme gesture of sharing. The problem was that he drank it black, she with cream. I have no idea how they worked it out.

We served dinner as soon as they returned from the bathroom. Sophie used Alexander's Ander name at least twenty times during the meal, and ate the chicken's back and neck to ensure that The Great One could eat three breasts. The devoted sheen never left her eyes, not even when I cornered her in the bedroom while she she was putting on her coat.

"You worship him, don't you?" I asked.

She smiled. "Yes. He makes love like God."

"Like a god?"

"No, like God." She collected her purse and the now deified Alex, wished me a happy birthday, and left.

How could I have a happy birthday living with a mere mortal?

"Benny," I confided while we washed the dishes, "Sophie says that Alex makes love like God."

"What does that mean—once every millennium?"

I ignored this. "Benny, do you love me?"

"Sure I do."

"Then worship me like Sophie worships Alex," I pleaded. "Just for five minutes. Just for my birthday."

"All right," he said. He sank to his knees and threw both arms around my legs. "You are a goddess. You are Venus. I will never leave you."

I didn't see how Alex endured it. "Get up," I sighed.

A serious depression was taking me over. Benny and I were not Great Lovers. Our pathetic passion was a sad flicker compared even to the eternal flame of Ozzie and Harriet, let alone to that of Sophie and Alexander-the-Greater-Than-You-Ever-Guessed. I told Benny so.

"Look," he said. "Every couple has a public relations department, and some work overtime. You know my brother Carlo? He married a woman who gained a hundred pounds in their first year of marriage. He didn't want to sleep with her any more. So, instead of losing weight, she put her diaphragm out in the bathroom in full view. She wanted their guests to see it and think that it was frequently used, always accessible."

"How bizarre."

"Well, it was more important to her that other people believed that they had a great sex life than for them to actually have a great sex life."

"If Sophie's diaphragm is in our bathroom, I'm going to throw up."

I spent the night dreaming about my sexual and romantic failings. If I were a real woman who signed Benny's name to my cards and called him Benito, he'd surely make love like God and see *Betrayal* without being coerced. It was all my fault for years of giving him the cement avocado. I didn't deserve to be loved; it was that simple.

"I'll make it all up to you," I whispered in his ear as he was waking up. "I'll make you the happiest man in the world, and I'll start by bringing you breakfast in bed." It was the only time other than his birthday that I'd offered to do such a thing.

"Wonderful," he said, eyes closed. "I want pancakes."

Nothing irritates me more than making pancakes (why hadn't he asked for eggs?) but as I was now a real woman, I would proceed to make him feel like a real man. Who knows? Perhaps then we could make godlike love. I was stirring pancake batter with what I hoped was religious zeal when the phone rang. It was Sophie sobbing to me that Alex, Alex without the Ander, was reconciling with his wife.

I had no idea what to say. It didn't really matter because she wasn't listening anyway, just yelping and crying. She finally hung up, promising to call me back when she was more coherent.

I sat back, cradling the phone in my lap, dazed.

"Where are my pancakes?" Benny yelled from the bedroom. "And bring me the paper," he added. "I promise that godlike sex awaits you."

I thought about maple syrup on the pillow case and grimaced. "Get up," I yelled back. "We're going out to breakfast." Why break tradition when every Sunday of our lives we went to the corner café for my eggs, his pancakes, and a thorough reading of the paper?

Benny was up and dressed in two minutes. "Is the honeymoon over?" he asked me, buttoning his shirt.

"Sophie's and Alex's is," I said. He looked surprised. "I'll tell you about it over breakfast," I promised, putting on my jacket.

"Okay," he said, thoughtfully. "But I meant *our* honeymoon. No breakfast in bed. Is it over?"

"Relax, Benito," I said, holding the door open for him. "I'll love you forever." I think I meant it, too.

14. Fighting

All through their passionate yet courtly courtship, Ann wondered when she and Jerry would have their first fight, and what would inspire it. She knew from experience that the catalyst could be anything from an inane political debate fueled by too much wine to the inevitable introduction of friends into their present nation of two ("Your friends don't like me because I'm not a professional." "Your friends don't know who's president.") to a real or imagined sexual betrayal.

Ann dreaded that first fight because she knew it would lay a premise for all the fights to come. One harsh word opened the door for a whole vocabularyful. The same held true for the first great sulk, or the first punitive silent treatment. Lying beside him in what should have been blissful tranquillity, Ann sighed deeply while Jerry slept. It was just a matter of time, she thought. She hoped, glancing about the serene quarters, that their first fight would not take place in her bedroom. Or his.

Ann loathed arguments with men more than her girlfriends Joyce and Beatrice did. The reason was simple: she had no brothers, and her father had never yelled at her. Unconditioned, she was reduced to Jell-O by a raised male voice. Joyce and Beatrice,

on the other hand, yelled back fearlessly. Their fathers had bellowed regularly, and their brothers spent their childhood beating
them up and reading their diaries aloud to the neighborhood.

Ann yelled back when pushed, but then always felt like a harpie.
If anyone ever heard her, she'd die of humiliation. She was horrified by the litany of stupidity that had passed her lips over her
years of arguing with men. Beatrice and Joyce assured her they
sounded just as irrational and shrill. "Don't feel guilty," they
instructed her. "Every woman has a harpie streak."

Along with the issue and the timing, Ann tried to predict the
location of their first fight. If not the sanctity of the bedroom,
where? She hoped it would not be in a restaurant. Eating while
fighting was almost impossible, and expensive as well. In her life,
the sparks had always started to fly just as she was being served
her entreé. She'd wept onto veal piccata more times than she
cared to remember, taking it home in a bag and being unable to
eat it the next day because of its unsavory connotations. She had
eventually lost her taste for capers altogether.

The worst aspect of a restaurant fight, however, was that it was
in public. Even when no voices were raised, she could always tell
when a couple was fighting by the quality of the silence between
them, punctuated with brittle remarks and a replenishing of wine.
She remembered going to the ladies' room at Giorgio's one evening, after struggling with her saltwater veal, and finding another
woman weeping in the lounge. "It's such a drag," the woman had
confided a little drunkenly, wiping her eyes. Ann loaned her a
squirt of Chanel Number Five.

She'd never, thank God, been abandoned in a restaurant as
Beatrice had. After hearing Beatrice's story, Ann never again left
the house without her own set of keys, two credit cards, and $25
in cash. Beatrice's date had risen in a huff and walked out. Quick-
witted, she tried to minimize her humiliation by smiling and
waving to his retreating back, as if this exit were by mutual,

amicable agreement, an emergency, perhaps, from which he'd soon return. Beatrice forced down the rest of her dinner, refused the cognac offered by an unknown man at the bar, and took a cab home. If it happened again, she'd told Ann and Joyce, she'd just bag dinner and accept the cognac gratefully.

Of course, Ann mused, adjusting the down comforter while Jerry snored, there was that slim possibility that they might never fight at all. But the only couple she knew who didn't fight were Rose and Vernon, and they seemed not to communicate on any level, hostile or otherwise. Looking at Jerry's handsome face, she tenderly stroked the bridge of his nose. She'd read somewhere that good sex was usually paid for with equally heated fights; if this were true, she and Jerry were in trouble. A couple had to be interested in each other to fight, and maybe in some way interested in the sport of fighting itself.

Her friend Joyce was a fighter who was inspired, she readily admitted, by seeing the film *Who's Afraid of Virginia Woolf?* "It made me like grand hostile gestures and saying pithy brutal things," she explained. One night Joyce and her husband were having their traditional post-party fight in the car ("Restaurant fights may be bad, but at least they can't send you through a windshield!") on the way home. Accused of flirting and of having too good a time, she pretended to throw her wedding ring out the car window into a gutter a block from their apartment. She had, in reality, slipped the ring into her pocket with her other hand, but her husband was properly deceived and spent half the night searching the gutter with a flashlight. "Was a woman ever meaner?" Joyce had asked.

Yes, Ann had been meaner, and all for the sake of expediency. She'd been mean to Donald, a boyfriend who'd started putting on weight during their relationship of three years. When Ann tired of a two-hour fight that wasn't going anywhere (and they never went anywhere; a couple could rotate the same three arguments for fifty years) she'd reduce him to silence by stating: "Donald, you're getting fat." This tactic was a last resort; she'd never have used it if Donald had a serious weight problem. Still, recalling it always made her feel guilty.

Donald lost weight, and one night they discovered a new fighting style while watching the late show on TV, as Fred Astaire sang "They Can't Take That Away from Me" to Ginger Rogers: "The way you wear your hat, the way you sip your tea, the memory of all that . . ." The next morning Donald discovered Ann had used his razor again after he'd repeatedly asked her not to. He sang to her: "The way you use my razor . . ." Ann responded immediately in perfect pitch: "The way you never clean the tub." They went on to sing their accusations back and forth, hampered only by the problem of keeping their complaints down to the right number of syllables. This ritual took some of the sting out of fighting—but not when they were breaking up. "The way I'm leaving you, the way I wasted three good years . . ."—those lines were too sour to sing.

Caressing Jerry's blond curly hair, Ann wondered if he could sing. Maybe their first fight would be musical; maybe they could add the element of dance. She was glad they weren't attorneys: "Point A: You're stupid. Point B: You're incredibly stupid. And in conclusion, I'm leaving you in Giorgio's to choke on your veal piccata . . ."

It was strange. The older she got the more she liked sex and the more she hated fighting. It used to take her a good week to get the toxins of sulk, silence, and verbal trespass out of her system; now it'd probably take ten days. She wasn't hearty like Joyce—could no more enact a wedding-ring–gutter-drama than she could throw a drink in a man's face (Beatrice had done this once at a party because it seemed like a good Bette Davis thing to do.) She doubted she even had the strength anymore to tell Donald he was fat.

And if she were to actually marry Jerry, Ann reflected, there'd be years of marital issues to fight about: house, money, whether or not to buy a VCR. And if they had children: more money, childrearing, diaper service or Pampers. And housework. In-laws. Professional competition. Thirty years of aborted dinners at Giorgio's. . . .

I can't sleep now, she thought, glancing at the clock. It was 3:30 in the morning and she was wide awake with trepidation. Silently, gingerly, she slipped on her chenille robe, tiptoed to the living room, poured herself a shot of brandy and turned the TV on low. Maybe there'd be a late movie on that could, in the spirit of Liz Taylor, Bette Davis, or Fred Astaire, teach her a new way to fight. Maybe the sound of the TV would wake Jerry, and her anxiety would be cured. Their first fight would be at 3:30 A.M., in her living room, and it would be over her insensitivity to his need for eight hours of sleep.

Comforted by this thought, Ann fell asleep on the couch.

15. Shrink to Fit

r. Ross, a gay therapist who counsels gay couples, once boasted to me that he could tell in the first five minutes of the first therapy session whether or not the marriage could be saved. "I jot down my prediction and ninety percent of the time I'm right."

My own relationship was disintegrating at the time, so I made Dr. Ross a proposition. "Come have dinner with George and me and tell me after the first course if I should leave him or not."

"I couldn't in good conscience make such a judgment," he said. "Why don't you two go to a straight therapist?"

"A man or a woman?" I asked.

"Oh, God—a woman, by all means. Straight men don't know what's going on."

"How do I get him to go?"

"Threaten to leave him if he doesn't."

"What if we go and the therapist takes his side?"

"They don't take sides."

"In their hearts they must."

"Listen, a good therapist can tell right away who's doing the emotional housework in a relationship. And in straight relationships it's almost always the same person who's doing the physical housework."

"In other words, the woman."

Dr. Ross gave me a hard look. "Well, who in your household makes a concerted effort to confront and solve marital problems? Who is the one who keeps saying: 'Let's talk about this.'?"

"I am."

"And who cleans the bathroom?"

"I get your point."

What I didn't get was who cleaned the bathroom in gay relationships, but rather than bother Dr. Ross about that I began to look for a therapist. Every woman I know has spent time in a therapist's office, either alone or with her mate, so I collected recommendations and made my choice: Dr. Goldstein, a woman in her sixties who emanated wisdom, compassion, and patience. At least this is what my friends swore was true, and this was how she sounded on the phone.

Surprisingly, George agreed we could use some counseling. "We're up to twenty fights a day," he said. "We'd better do *something.*" He just couldn't agree on a time.

"She has Tuesday at four open," I said, referring to my notes.

"I can't get away from work."

"How about Friday at three?"

"That's no good either."

"Monday at six? You can say you're leaving early for a doctor's appointment. It *is* a doctor's appointment." This was the end of the available time slots; good shrinks are in high demand.

"Nope! Sorry," he said, leaving the room.

"Saturday at ten? Sunday at eight?" I yelled after him. These times were fictitious, but I wanted to see exactly how strong this classic case of resistance was. He declined them all.

"Don't you want to go?" I asked.

"Sure I do. Just find a good time."

I ignored Dr. Ross's advice and did not threaten to leave. After all, I wanted to see a therapist because I didn't *want* to leave

George; I wanted to *fix* him, like a malfunctioning appliance. Wasn't that the point of therapy—to soothe the psychic wounds, trace them to their source, and hopefully abolish their chances of coming back?

I called my girlfriend Sarah. "The resistance is like a brick tidal wave. What should I do?"

"Are you two still speaking?"

"Monosyllabically."

"Have you resorted to the long letters yet?"

Evidently not. "What do you mean?"

"Toward the end of our marriage I used to write Sam four-page letters twice a week. I'd lie beside him all night, unable to sleep or speak, then get up at five A.M. and write these long epistles, listing my grievances, repenting for my sins, explaining my interpretation of our last five years together. Then I'd put the letter on top of his briefcase so he could read it at work."

"Did he write back?"

"No, he said he wasn't a good correspondent."

"Did he answer you at all?"

"No, he literally told me he couldn't think of anything to say. I realized then that there was nothing to work with, that I couldn't save the marriage by myself, and I left."

My heart sank, froze, and flipped over all at the same time. I refused to believe Dr. Ross's indictment of straight men—that they didn't know what was going on. Did *I* know what was going on? What *was* going on? I called Sheldon, an old friend, a married friend, and the straightest of men.

"Sheldon, you and Lucy went through couple therapy, didn't you?"

"I had to drag her in kicking and screaming."

"*You* dragged *her?*"

"Oh, yeah. She was terrified. She was sure the therapist and I would gang up on her."

"Did you?"

"Hardly. Lucy and I separated after four sessions and then the therapist asked her out."

"Are you serious? Did she go out with him?"

"Yes, I'm serious, and no, she didn't. In fact, we reconciled shortly after that."

"Would you say therapy helped your marriage?"

"In a weird way. Lucy hated the therapist even more than she hated me. I started looking good to her again. And you know I've always loved Lucy." Sheldon proceeded to hum the theme song to the *I Love Lucy* show, a habit he's been fond of for seven years. It's too endearing to be irritating. "Everything's hunky-dunk now. You should try it."

"I'm trying to try it, but George won't go. Maybe it's because Dr. Goldstein's a woman and he's afraid of being outnumbered. Like Lucy was."

"Yeah, maybe that's it. Pick a man. Pick *our* man. You can always date him yourself if your relationship doesn't improve."

"Thanks a lot."

It occurred to me that it might be the considerable expense of therapy that frightened George the most, so I offered to pay for it myself.

"That's ridiculous," he said. "You can't afford it."

"It's a mere pittance compared to what it costs to live alone," I reminded him. Following Sarah's example, I wrote him a four-page letter, one page of which listed possible dates and times for our appointment. I asked him to check off the ones he thought he might be able to keep. A week later I found the list untouched.

"I can't get off work," he kept saying.

I knew he didn't even like his job. "If your mother died, would your boss let you attend her funeral?" I asked. He conceded he probably would. "Well, our relationship is in the intensive care unit, and every time you refuse to make this appointment, you're yanking on the plug." This was probably a stupid analogy; George didn't like his mother either.

What *did* he like? Not his job, not his mother, certainly not me, and not even another woman. I called Sheldon the next Saturday after a domestic fight that had led to a chilling revelation.

"Let's meet at the taquería," he suggested. Sheldon likes to fit in a *carnitas* burrito whenever he can.

We sat at a tiny table cluttered with beer bottles and dirty napkins. The scent of fresh cilantro was heady to me as I told Sheldon, "I figured it out this morning. He's in love with his own pain. It's his best friend; he wants nothing to interfere with it."

Sheldon didn't say anything. I kicked him under the table. "Talk to me!" I pleaded.

"I'm just glad you finally figured it out," he said.

"What? That he's in love with his own pain? Did you already know that?" I hate it that you always finally break up with someone for reasons your friends recognized long ago.

"And there's another thing. George isn't big on forgiveness. Remember when I didn't return his screwdriver on time? He was mad at me for two years. Why do you think he's going to allow *you* any margin for error?"

The writing was on the wall just as sure as the hot sauce was smeared across Sheldon's bristly chin. I wouldn't need Dr. Ross to make his five-minute assessment. I wouldn't need any more writing paper. What I would need, though, was to visit Dr. Goldstein at the first opportunity. If you can't get your partner to the therapist, make sure not to cancel that first appointment. You'll need it more than ever.

16. In Sickness and in Health

When friends asked Antoinette how she fell in love with Larry, she explained it would never have happened if he had not lived across the street during her Year of Mishaps. The first mishap was orthopedic; she broke her left ankle and wore a walking cast for three weeks. To her chagrin, she broke it not while skiing or dancing, but rather in the literally pedestrian course of getting off a bus.

Larry, who had three brothers and two sisters and knew all about orthopedic mishaps, brought groceries to her third-floor apartment and always remembered fresh artichokes and lemons. He traded cars with her until the cast came off, because she drove a standard shift and he an automatic. But his most impressive feat was in teaching her to bathe; he loaned her a giant trash bag and a plastic lawn chair and told her she could get squeaky clean by sitting beneath the shower head with her leg protectively bagged. Larry had had knee surgery once, and knew whereof he spoke.

It was a cumbersome arrangement, particularly because Antoinette and Larry were not intimate and could not collaborate on arranging her naked body on the lawn chair. Larry called instructions through the bathroom door, reminding her to wrap two rubber bands at the top of the trash bag. Antoinette called back

her reports of progress—dropping the soap and finding it again—
and hobbled out thirty minutes later wrapped in a jumbo-size
yellow towel.

Though she insisted she could go by herself, Larry insisted even
harder that he accompany her to the hospital for the removal of
her cast. The first moment she stood on the newly liberated foot,
she was grateful. She felt like jelly; she felt old. The doctor offered
her a cane and an Ace bandage; she took the bandage and leaned
on Larry.

Antoinette reasoned it was the stress of the ankle injury that left
her vulnerable to the most obnoxious cold she'd ever suffered.
Two days after her cast came off, she was a red, teary pulp buried
in Kleenex. Again, she was embarrassed by the unremarkable
nature of her ailment; the common cold was a dull affliction. Hers,
though, seemed uncommonly tenacious; Larry thought it merged
with flu, because she couldn't get out of bed for a week. Every
evening after work Larry climbed the three floors to her apartment laden with supplies: liquids of all variety, aspirin and cold
pills, and magazines both erudite and trashy. He taught her to
steam her face over a tea kettle to open her nasal passages, then
gave her his linen handkerchief and politely looked away. Antoinette knew she looked pathetic, but he never seemed to notice.
The cold, she later realized, began to improve the night he fed
her homemade chicken soup and massaged her feet while they
watched *Dark Victory* on TV. The cathartic sobs *Dark Victory*
evoked were, Larry told her, good for healing.

Antoinette was amazed Larry did not catch her cold; he told
her he was annoyingly healthy, that he'd lucked into a strong
constitution. Once well, she expressed her gratitude for his medical attentions by inviting him to dinner at her favorite Italian
restaurant, all on her.

Thrilled to be able to taste real food again, she exhorted him
to order whatever he wanted. Soon their table was covered with
platters of pasta, veal, and shellfish laced with fresh tomato and

garlic, the best garlic bread in the city, and an expensive bottle of red wine.

It was the shellfish, Larry surmised, that made Antoinette throw up in his car on the way home. He'd always been allergic to shellfish and had eaten the veal saltimbocca instead. He explained the violent but short-lived nature of food poisoning to Antoinette, who leaned out the car window, humiliated. Looking only straight ahead, he handed her a small grocery bag from his back seat and urged her to use it. Even in her gastrointestinal misery, Antoinette could appreciate the wisdom of using the bag —it cleverly eliminated the visual and olfactory effects of the whole unhappy process. She continued to use it as Larry guided her up the three floors to her apartment, where she stayed in her bathroom for two hours, alternately weeping on the toilet seat and laying her face against the cool tile floor.

When she emerged, hesitant and drained, Larry was quietly reading a magazine on her couch, a quartered lemon on a dish beside him. He told her he'd called the restaurant and screamed at the manager, and that she was to go to bed immediately and suck on a lemon wedge if nausea returned. He waited to make sure the worst was over; it was after 1:00 A.M. when he went home.

Antoinette got into bed and pondered the intimacy of throwing up in front of a man, something she'd never done before. How repulsive, she thought. Yet Larry didn't seem repulsed. An English professor once told her class that every woman's closet had a nurse's uniform hanging in it. Antoinette thought that she might be the exception, but realized she'd found a man with that same supposedly female nursing instinct. Before she drifted off, she noticed Larry had turned her electric blanket on to "low" for her.

Antoinette's fourth mishap was a tragedy—the accidental death of a friend she'd known in college. The news came to her from the east coast, sending her spinning to a place she'd never been before: sleepless nights, unexpected panics, terror and inconsolable loss.

Larry said very little; mostly he sat with her, took her on long walks, touched her shoulder when it seemed it needed to be touched. He helped her write a note to her friend's parents; he urged her to call him when she awoke in the night stricken with thoughts of mortality. It was Antoinette's first experience with death; all her feelings were surprises. Larry told her he'd lost a sister to leukemia ten years ago; he'd learned then the curative powers of long walks. She leaned on him, and called him often.

Antoinette changed the name of her "Year of Mishaps" to her "Year of Trauma and Recovery." She felt leveled, then uplifted; diminished, then enlarged. She began to look in earnest for that fabled nurse's uniform hanging in her own closet; perhaps it was hidden behind all those colorful dresses.

As she later told her inquisitive friends, if anyone could help her to find it, she knew that someone would be Larry.

Breaking Up

17. Heartbreak Hotel

It isn't fair. I was just beginning to recover from divorcing Dr. Infidel when I inadvertently became the proprietress of Heartbreak Hotel. He ran off one year ago with Nurse Vivacious, leaving me the three-bedroom house and Paisano, the old, tired, golden retriever.

I have to admit I did not cope well. I spent six months wallowing in self-pity, revenge fantasies, and varying degrees of alienation. I dated inappropriate men, I watched too much TV, I even poured Chianti into Paisano's water dish one night because I didn't want to drink alone.

But I got better. I emerged from my stupor and enrolled in a French literature class and intermediate aerobics. I was on the fourth volume of Proust's *Remembrance of Things Past* (in French, thank you) and I could run in place for fifteen minutes without passing out. I apologized to Paisano for trying to turn him into a co-alcoholic. In short, I got off self-destruct. Then Elaine called.

"Eddie's left me," she sobbed into the phone. "He left me for our tax consultant. I hate professional women."

It wasn't much of a surprise. Eddie was the kind of man who

always tried to get the waitress's phone number while Elaine was in the ladies' room.

"I hate him, I hate our apartment, and most of all I hate being alone. Could I stay with you and Paisano for a while? Until I feel stronger?"

What could I say to a woman who had given me the name of the best vet in the city when Paisano had mange? "My home is your home," I said. After all, I had stayed with my mother the first three weeks after the disclosure of Dr. Infidel's infidelity. Elaine's mother lived in Florida, so I would fill in.

I was putting fresh sheets on Elaine's bed when the phone rang again. It was uncannily synchronistic, which synchronicity always is.

It was my friend Pam. She was leaving Howard. "I finally decided to cut my losses," she said. Her voice did not have the hysteria of Elaine's, just the flat tone of the resigned. "The thing is, in order to leave him, I have to go somewhere. Can I stay with you?"

That's when I heard Elvis Presley singing the sad words of "Heartbreak Hotel."

"Why are everyone's marriages going belly up at the same time?" I asked her, explaining about Elaine and Eddie and the tax consultant.

Pam pretended not to be comforted by the news. "I guess the warranties ran out," she said.

"Misery loves company," I offered lamely.

"Party hearty," she deadpanned, and hung up.

They arrived at my door at the same time, Elaine dressed defiantly in cheerful white, Pam, who had defiantly left her husband, in a bathrobe and slippers. Paisano, teeming with boisterous canine sympathy, lunged for Pam, licking her face. This made her cry.

"Why doesn't he feel sorry for *me?*" Elaine asked. "I'm the one who got left."

"You're dressed too well," I said.

"The dumped have to dress well," she explained. "We have to have *some* dignity. Sorry about this particular outfit, though," she apologized.

During my Negative Phase I had forbidden my friends to wear white in my presence—it was too medical. "I'm sane now," I said. "You can wear stethoscopes around your neck and it won't bother me. I don't have hatred in my heart any more." I knew how inane I sounded, but it was a necessary part of the Positive Phase.

"Don't worry," said Elaine, "I have enough hatred in my heart for both of us."

She did, too. The first thing she did when she got inside was mount a homemade Eddie dart board on my living-room wall. Instead of risking a miss by throwing the darts, she stood six inches away from his photo and thrust them into his nostrils and eyeballs. "I wish they made dart boards that bleed," she said. "Hey, maybe I should patent that idea and make a million dollars. Then I can hire a hit man to kill Eddie and that heinous tax bitch."

Pam looked at the dart board incredulously and said, "You are really sick."

"Me? Sick? If Howard had left *you,* you'd be just as sick!"

They looked to me as if I, their proprietress of Heartbreak Hotel, should decide who was sick and who wasn't. "It's a harmless ventilation of hostile feelings," I said idiotically. I was glad Paisano couldn't speak, as only he knew about the Dr. Infidel and Nurse Vivacious voodoo dolls that I'd made and then murdered with my own hostile hands.

"It's already seven," Elaine said, turning from the pockmarked Eddie. "Why don't we go out to dinner?"

"Fine," I said. "There's a good Japanese place down the street." Along with Proust and exercise, I had discovered the calming effects of raw fish and rice. Food for the serenely positive.

"I am far too upset for gentle yin-yang cuisine," said Elaine. "I need carbohydrates and spices. I need spaghetti in marinara sauce and lots of drinks." As she spoke, visions of my Negative Phase menu flashed before me: mountains of pasta and gallons of wine, resulting in a ten-pound weight gain. I knew there was a reason I'd taken up aerobics.

"I can't go out," Pam whimpered. "I'm wearing a bathrobe."

"So take it off," Elaine said, impatiently.

"Why should I? I think I'll wear it the rest of my life. You two go without me—I'm too depressed to eat anyway."

"Too depressed to eat?" Elaine blurted. "Food's the only dependable thing in life. It never betrays you!" Paisano, a voracious and indiscriminate eater, barked affirmatively. "See? Paisano knows," she said, throwing her arms around his furry, overweight neck. He was thrilled by the attention. "Wonderful Paisano. I wish I'd married a dog, at least they're faithful."

"Now I *really* can't eat," Pam said, disgusted at this display.

"What if we order in?" I asked Pam, and she brightened. Aha. It wasn't lack of appetite; it was post-breakup agoraphobia. When I'd stayed with my mother for those first three weeks, I left her house maybe twice. I felt as if a neon sign saying MY HUSBAND LEFT ME FOR ANOTHER WOMAN was growing out of my head. I was also afraid of the very real possibility of running into Dr. Infidel and Nurse Vivacious somewhere. And I harbored, for that time, a sincere hatred for all humanity and didn't see why I should interact with any of it. Nor did Pam; even though she was the one leaving Howard, she felt stigmatized by a failed marriage.

"Okay, let's order pizza," Elaine said, grabbing the phone. She ordered a jumbo giant with everything on it plus double on the pepperoni and two bottles of red wine.

"Couldn't we get salads too?" I suggested gently after she hung up.

"What's the point?" she yelled, scaring Paisano. "What's the point of eating fresh greens and trying to be healthy? I steamed broccoli and broiled chicken breasts for Eddie for years! I made a fresh green salad every night! I never used anything from a can or a package and there was always fresh fruit on the table! And where did it get me? He left me for a tax consultant! Well, forget it! I've had it with good health and following the rules—I'm eating nitrites from now on!" She burst into tears. Pam did too, then padded over to the couch in her furry slippers and put her arms around Elaine. Paisano, unable to cry, drooled consolingly on Elaine's knees. And I, who hadn't cried in six months, suddenly remembered that was all I did in my Negative Phase and bawled like a baby.

Great, I thought, dropping a box of Kleenex on the coffee table. Just great.

=====

I woke up with my first hangover since entering my Positive Phase. We'd stayed up until two, drinking wine and philosophizing on the death of love. I staggered out of my bedroom and tried to open the bathroom door.

"I'm taking a bath," came Pam's muffled voice.

Defeated, I went to the kitchen to make tea. Elaine was still sleeping, as was Paisano, who'd thrown up a slice of pepperoni pizza at midnight. I drank tea, ate toast, and tried the bathroom again.

"It's so warm in here," came Pam's voice. "Like the womb."

I turned on the TV to see how Jane Pauley and Maria Shriver were doing. I'd give Pam five more minutes. At the commercial, I knocked on the door again.

"Hydrotherapy," she said.

I remembered now that I was not only afraid of leaving the house after Dr. Infidel left me, I'd been afraid to leave the bathtub. I used to drink steaming mugs of hot water, brandy, and lemon while I sat in the bubbles, enveloping myself inside and out in warm, lulling liquid. It *was* therapy. But why did she have to do it at 7:30 in the morning? Probably because she couldn't sleep, another post-breakup problem.

I sighed and dressed. Just this once I'd be Saint Heartbreak and go to work dirty.

I called home at noon to see how my guests were faring. Elaine answered.

"Did you find your house keys?" I asked. "I left a set on the coffee table."

"Thanks. I was going to make another set for Pam, but she's never leaving the house, so she doesn't need them."

"Is she still in the tub?"

"She came out to watch *The Young and the Restless* and then went back in. She has quite a capacity for suffering, considering she's the one who left."

"What are you doing?"

"I went out to breakfast and gave the short-order cook my phone number. I mean, your phone number."

Right—the inappropriate man syndrome. A date with the door-knob, as long as it raises the damaged self-esteem. At least it was better than digging through the old boyfriend file and trying to rekindle long-dead flames.

"How's Paisano?"

"Better. He stopped throwing up."

"Good. I'm going to my exercise class and I'll be home at seven. Want me to bring you anything?"

"Is heroin on special anywhere?"

===

It wasn't, so I brought home a chicken, carrots, onions, a bottle of Chablis and three boxes of Kleenex. Pam, Elaine, and Paisano were waiting for me in the living room, which was beginning to feel like the lobby. Pam had switched from her bathrobe to one of mine and sat in an armchair looking pale and very clean. She was reading *People* magazine. Elaine wore a red dress and seven pounds of eye makeup and was reading Lana Turner's autobiography.

"I always read dumb magazines when I'm upset," Pam said defensively.

"Lana Turner is the only person whose love life is stupider than mine," said Elaine.

I thought of Proust and how much I hadn't read last night. "I'm making chicken soup for dinner," I said. "It will make us all feel better."

"I have a date," Elaine said. "Thanks anyway."

"I'm not hungry," whimpered Pam.

"Well, I'm not making soup for one," I said. This meant dining on English muffins and tuna fish, a depressing habit I'd tried to get rid of. Pizza and tuna—these were bad signs.

"The bathroom's free now," Pam offered apologetically. I raced in to take my shower. When I came back Elaine had left on her date with the short-order cook, and Pam was watching *Valley of the Dolls* on cablevision. I thought of Proust; I thought of a documentary on the war in Vietnam that was on the public broadcasting station.

"It helps to watch movies about people whose lives are more wrecked than your own," Pam felt the need to explain.

Didn't I know it. "Tuna fish?" I offered, heading for the kitchen, knowing I was too undisciplined to go to my room and read Proust. My response to trashy TV was Pavlovian—I couldn't wait to see Patty Duke.

"No thanks," she said. "I would like a glass of wine, though. A big one."

===

Elaine checked back into Heartbreak Hotel at seven in the morning. "That was a very big mistake," she said, stepping over the sleeping Paisano, entering her bedroom and closing the door.

===

I decided to skip my French class that night because I'd lost two nights' reading and was embarrassingly behind. I wanted to go home and catch up, but was afraid of being lured into another evening of depressed bathrobe inactivity: drink, gossip, and TV.

But maybe I could get around to making the chicken soup. And I was curious about Elaine's date.

They were arguing about her date when I got home.

"What did you expect?" Pam chided. "How could you even think of seeing another man five seconds after Eddie left?

"I thought it would cheer me up."

They were drinking martinis straight up. I couldn't believe they'd found the ancient shaker that Dr. Infidel had left behind in the bowels of our kitchen. Actually, the martinis looked rather elegant in their chilled glasses. I poured one for myself.

"Really, Elaine," Pam continued. "I don't know how you can even think about men. I don't think I'll ever date again."

"You won't if you keep wearing that bathrobe," Elaine warned.

"What was wrong with the short-order cook?" I asked, eating my olive. "Aside from his being a total stranger who might have been an axe murderer with AIDS?"

"He had a copy of *Hustler* in his living room."

Pam almost lost her martini.

"And that's not the worst part," Elaine said, hurling a dart with her free hand into her husband's forehead. "His name was Edward."

We shared a superstitious silence.

"What about you?" Pam said, turning to me. "Do you think you'll ever date again?"

"What makes you think I don't date now?" I asked. I looked at Paisano, again relieved that he could not tell them that since I'd stopped dating inappropriate men, I'd stopped, period.

"I think I need a cigarette," I said, suddenly panicked. Damn. Proust and aerobics had kept me free of panic for a while, and I had made a point of never thinking about love or the future.

Elaine held out her Marlboros, but I waved them away and took one of Pam's unfiltered Camels instead. "These are worse for you," I explained.

The chicken remained uncooked in the refrigerator, and we

smoked and drank the night away, ordering another pizza at ten. It sounds implausible, but I think Paisano was sending me rueful looks.

If he wasn't, he should have been; I was in sad shape. I went to aerobics the next night but was too tired to keep up. The rest of my French class had moved on to volume five. My lungs hurt from smoking Camels. The rotting chicken had to be thrown into the garbage. I started using the Eddie dart board, pretending it was Dr. Infidel and Nurse Vivacious in alternate rounds. I realized I still hated them, that beneath my positive veneer was a morass of maladjustment. I became snappy, irritable; I pounded on the bathroom door and told Pam to get out of the tub so I could get into it myself.

I think they call it a relapse.

———

I awoke to find Pam actually wearing a skirt and blouse and Elaine with a normal amount of eye makeup. They had set the kitchen table and cooked a sane breakfast.

"Poached eggs," Elaine said soothingly, putting two in front of me.

Pam poured my tea solicitously, then buttered my toast.

"Staying here has been great for us, but not too healthy for you," Elaine said. "So we've made some decisions. Pam can't go back to her place because Howard insists on staying there paying millions of dollars in rent and being wounded. I don't want to go back to my apartment because it's too much memory lane."

Memory lane: maybe that was why I'd had this relapse. Was it wise to remain in the house where I'd lived happily and then unhappily with Dr. Infidel? Jane Austen said something to the effect that one should not love a place the less for having suffered in it, but then she'd never been married. Or divorced.

"So we're getting a new place and rooming together," Elaine said.

I tried not to look surprised. I didn't think Pam and Elaine got along all that well. But misery is bonding.

"We're getting a place with two bathrooms," Pam said quickly. "Anyway, we're too poor to live alone."

"What if you reconcile with your husbands?"

"That would only happen if I killed that tax bitch and if Howard got a brain transplant," Elaine assured me.

"What if one of you gets a lover and the other one gets cranky?"

They looked at me as if I was crazy. "I've had my short-order cook for the year," Elaine said.

"I can buy my own *Hustler* if I want to," said Pam.

They looked as though they had taken care of everything. They'd packed their suitcases, laundered their sheets and towels, and were on their way.

"You run a great hotel," they shouted to me from Elaine's Honda.

===

I have to say, their manners improved with their moods. When I got home that night a dozen red roses with a profuse thank-you note were waiting. My house was back to normal: no more over-flowing ashtrays or overturned wineglasses, no empty pizza boxes smeared with tomato sauce, no Eddie dart board.

Paisano and I settled on the couch to read Proust, my French-English dictionary at my side. Then the phone rang. It was Brian, a math genius I've known since college. His marriage had just exploded into a million pieces.

"I ran into Pam and Elaine today," he said, "and they told me you were running sort of a Heartbreak Hotel, a halfway house for the romantically displaced. Lots of room, good water pressure. Do you allow male guests?"

Oh, sure. I'd be in the Betty Ford Center in a month.

"Sorry, Brian, but I don't think I'm really cut out for the hotel business." He sighed. I sighed. Then I remembered that Brian was a man, and not an entirely inappropriate one. I knew the newly separated are almost disfunctional, but it wouldn't hurt to see him. If he'd ask.

"That's too bad," he said. "But God, I'm miserable. If I took you to dinner, would you let me tell you how miserable I am?"

"Of course!" I said gaily, shoving Proust aside. "Just don't bring any dart boards." He promised he wouldn't if I promised to explain over dinner what that meant. I promised, hung up, kissed Paisano and dressed for dinner.

18. Cuisine of a Failed Romance

pring: The first time I had him over to the apartment I served both duck and veal pâté (options were important) and chilled two champagne glasses. As promised, he brought the champagne, icy and expensive, and he uncorked and poured it without any spillage save that of his beautiful smile. His smile and the life in his black eyes radiated everywhere, placing me in a quasi-paralysis. During each of our early pâté and champagne rituals I literally could not speak to him for the first twenty minutes after his arrival. I am a talker and yet could not talk in his presence until half the champagne was gone and the pâté nibbled at: I was that enthralled.

Food is a useful prism through which to view the progress of an affair. It is at least as useful a barometer as any other.

The first time I had him to dinner it was important that everything be fresh, innovative, spontaneous and lovely. I chose linguini and fresh clams. I gambled on the prospect that he would love fish, relish the ritual of detaching the clams from their possessive shells and admire the tenderness of fresh pasta. It worked. He was impressed. It was an edible love project—not without design, certainly, but it comforted and seduced.

Weeks flew by. He worked long hours; mealtimes were erratic.

He loved fresh, marinated things, and was a vinegar fan, a proponent of the sour. I marinated huge bowls full of vegetables to be eaten cold on his arrival, usually around 10:00 P.M. We sopped up the marinades with French bread. "You eat like me," he would say, in awed admiration. He confided that his previous girlfriend had been gastronomically blocked, afraid of most of the major food groups. Our taste buds, he said, were in accord.

One afternoon a male friend of long standing came over and watched patiently while I finished cooking vegetables. I cut and steamed each batch separately; from steamer to cold-water bath to colander they would go: cauliflower, zucchini, a few sweet red peppers, the occasional lima bean, mushrooms if they had looked promising that day. All ended up in a huge glass bowl in layers like those of an archaeological dig, to bathe a while in olive oil and a good red wine vinegar.

"I wish someone would love me like that," my friend said wistfully, seeing the plethora of color and texture enter the refrigerator under its plastic wrap. "Someone will," I assured him, while listening closely to this male wish for female nurturing. Food was the way to the male heart. It really did have power.

======

Summer: We moved in together after four months of courtship. I introduced him to veal and Marsala (or Madeira, whichever I spotted on the shelf first).

"You have good food sensibilities," he would say to me, watching me make the salad dressing. Only butter lettuce existed for us and no bottled dressing would be tolerated. Salad was a nightly expectation, and it sat on the dinner plate next to the rest of the meal—no segregation here. "Salads should sit next to their dinner partners," he agreed with me.

Feeding him was thrilling to me. I think it was because he had the sensibilities of a social worker (and, indeed, worked as one) and was a volunteer on the suicide hotline: He nurtured others every day. It was a joy to feed a giver, it was a joy to sit across from a man who did not discuss his business deals and did not know or care if he was tan or not.

I learned from him, too: black beans and ham hocks—the cheapest pot of heaven in the world; ceviche served in the shape of upside-down champagne glasses (the fish can be in the lime juice only six hours, he admonished—after that it becomes "over-cooked"); and the mysteries of coffee, which I didn't usually drink.

We discovered breakfast together—sometimes in bed, some-times not: sprouted wheat toast with sweet butter and grated feta cheese. We felt that no one else in San Francisco was having a breakfast like ours, but, as I claimed from the start, we had similar food sensibilities (and not always popular ones—our friends looked askance when we ordered calf's liver in restaurants). The gentle egg (this became its permanent name) was our ideal break-fast; next to the feta toast it was a scrambled soft yellow mass that soothed weekend nerves.

=====

Fall: Cohabitation continued, although shared meals, graced by tablecloths, wine and candles, decreased gradually.

"I need to eat less at night," he told me. His hours were late and his commute was long, and eating lighter made gastronomic and health sense. But what about the evening ritual, the exchange of work terrors and gossip and, on wonderful occasions, philosoph-ical airs? I kept making salads. In reputation, at any rate, salads are light. "Eating makes me tired—I just want to go to bed." All right, I agreed. I would eat alone and have something "light" for him when he got home. Then to bed, for sleep and quiet and solitude.

My garlic press and my wire whisks began gathering dust. I started buying barbecued chickens—splashed with an interesting vinegar they were more than fine—and a reasonable Italian wine. Sometimes I'd bring home won-ton soup from a nearby restaurant and we'd have—at different times—hot glass bowls full of Chinese nourishment. But other kinds of nourishment were on the wane.

Food separatism is easy to spot—it resembles different bedtimes.

═══

Winter: Barometers don't need literal translation. Anyone who eats or loves or who has longed to combine these two pleasures knows what happened. We parted ways, sadly, stupidly, in all the confused defeat in which such separations are made. I am looking upon the vista of single-unit cooking again.

I have done it before and know how it works: many artichokes and game hens, and muffins with unhappy toppings. Eggs play a high part in single life, not a gentle egg, certainly, and their ironic metaphor is too ridiculous to spell out. There are frozen foods now that promise slimness, perhaps eternal youth and/or immortality, and they involve no dishes. They seem to be growing in popularity as the U.S. population lives alone more and more literally. So life will be simpler now, grocery bags lighter and dinner candles unnecessary. One less egg to fry, as the song says. One less yolk to break.

19. Band-Aid* Affair

I once suffered the stupidity and misfortune of tearing the ligaments in my ankle. When the cast came off, I graduated to an elastic ankle supporter. It made me feel almost healed, imparting the same confidence as do bicycle training wheels. I wanted to wear it forever, because it made this injured portion of myself feel protected. When I did forsake my elastic band, it was with some trepidation; I envisioned my weakened ankle giving out in crowded intersections with brakeless tour buses heading my way. Later, as is usual with any human malady, I forgot that I'd ever been hurt.

Two months after tearing the metaphorical ligaments of my own heart, I foraged through my medicine cabinet looking for a Band-Aid for a grated finger. (Never go near a kitchen when you're upset; you end up julienned and broiled.) I found a "junior sheer strip" and wrapped it around my wound.

"As God is my witness, I'll never cook again," I vowed to my own finger, thinking for a moment that I was Scarlett O'Hara just before the intermission in *Gone With the Wind.* Then, impulsively, I unwrapped another Band-Aid and applied it to a larger

*BAND-AID is a registered trademark of Johnson & Johnson.

wound, my broken heart. It shone like the red (actually, flesh-toned) badge of courage atop my green sweater. "Not big enough," I decided next, reaching for a big square patch. I knew I needed industrial-sized healing.

At first I attributed my Band-Aid experiment to the derangement of living alone; just another unwitnessed activity like grating one's finger and reciting Scarlett O'Hara soliloquies. But the next morning I dressed for work, had my morning cry and found myself once again in search of that box of Band-Aids. I selected a standard size (the patch was too ostentatious—after all, he hadn't *died*) and smoothed it against my heart. I felt instantaneously better. As thin and flimsy as it was, my Band-Aid stood between the injured part of myself and the abrasive outside world. I remembered, then, my once-devastated ankle.

What I forgot, of course, was that the Band-Aid was visible to other people, and that it looked eccentric indeed stuck to my clothing.

"What's on your chest?" Beverly, a woman at work, asked me as I collected my morning mail.

"My heart hurts," I explained.

She stared at my left breast; it made me nervous. "So does mine," she confessed. "Do you have an extra?"

It so happened that I'd packed a couple of spares in case my original fell off, or in case I became inordinately unhappy during the day and required a second and third Band-Aid as reinforcement. I took one from my purse, unwrapped it and pressed it lightly to Beverly's chest. I knew intuitively that she wanted me to do it for her; the brokenhearted like to be tended. It's like having your mother put Vicks Vaporub on your five-year-old chest and under your five-year-old nose—you feel as if your guardian angel has finally remembered your phone number, and has come to envelop you in elastic ankle supporters, Band-Aids, and whatever else you need.

"Feel better?" I asked Beverly, standing back from my work.

"Don't laugh, but I do."

Word got around the office that I possessed, if not a cure, at least a temporary balm for heartache. People knocked on my office door, asking for medical attention. I never advised them to buy their own Band-Aids; I knew they had to be administered by another heartbreak victim in order to be effective. Within two weeks, half of the people in my office were sporting pink rectangles on their upper bodies. I hadn't realized before how invisible and constant heartbreak is.

"You, Ed?" I exclaimed, when the office womanizer showed up for treatment. "You have a wounded heart?"

"Why not?" he asked, petulantly. "Men have feelings too, you know."

"Ha!" erupted Beverly, who was just behind my office door. Ed flinched. I touched his arm reassuringly and reached in my bottom drawer for the Band-Aids.

"I turn away no one," I said, feeling like Mother Teresa as I peeled away the protective strip.

"How about a drink after work?" he asked.

"You don't understand, Ed," I said, patiently. "Let me explain a broken heart to you. You can tell when it's truly broken because you can't use it. It's in the repair shop. Get it? It doesn't work. It's getting fixed. Like . . . " I tried to think of something Ed would comprehend, which was hard because I knew he considered twenty minutes an adequate recovery time between love affairs. "Like your BMW, okay? When it's in the shop getting a new clutch, you stay at home, right?"

"Are you nuts? I take cabs."

"Give that back," I demanded, tearing off his Band-Aid. "You're not suffering."

"If you were a real woman, you'd get over this stupid heartbreak and get on with life," he sneered. "Or at least let me buy you a drink."

"Buy your BMW a drink," I sneered back.

Maybe this Band-Aid business was getting out of hand. Maybe we were all too influenced by symbolism, I thought. But I couldn't let go of it yet for two reasons: First, it was too good a conversation piece. When I explained to men at parties why I ruined a simple black dress with a Band-Aid, they'd regard me with what almost resembled respect. They'd start speaking quietly, freshening my drink, reciting their own heartbreak story. My Band-Aid was an emotional weather vane that warned: "I'm a wreck, but I came to this party anyway. Let's exchange safe pleasantries. If you're a wreck, too, I'll give you a Band-Aid of your own."

The second reason for hanging on to my Band-Aid was more basic: My heart still hurt. Unlike Ed, I needed more than a few minutes to mourn my loss, assess the damage and court the curative powers of solitude and quiet. I knew I'd have to taper off slowly.

I went from the standard size to the junior strip, the kind you wear on grated fingertips. I started skipping days. Then I just wore it on Fridays which, because they launched weekends, were hard days for me. And one morning I woke up and felt considerably better. I retired my box of Band-Aids to a remote corner of the medicine cabinet—in fact, next to my long-discarded ankle supporter.

I didn't, of course, throw either item away. I'm exhilarated to be whole again, but not so crazy as to think it will be an uninterrupted state.

20. Dignity Along the Way

I admit, with some chagrin, to having founded the Irate Celibates Club several years ago. This was, needless to say, during a romantic dry spell. To sweeten the bitterness, unmated friends of both genders and I formed a club whose sole prerequisite for joining was the harboring of at least as much ire as celibacy. One could not be a complacent celibate, nor could one be just generally irate. One had to be specifically furious about not frolicking on the beach with Mr. Right (or Ms. Right, or, for the ambitious, Dr. Right.) We'd have impromptu meetings and compare heartbreak stories: "My Most Degrading Date" or "Why I've Given It Up at Twenty-Five." It was amateur theater, it was hilarious, and it made otherwise empty evenings full and rich.

Homophobia may be too strong a term, but I suspect that it well describes what the women in the Irate Celibates experienced. Because our city teemed with gay men, it grew easier and easier to blame our arid Saturday nights on their preoccupation with each other. The logic of this complaint is obviously nil; gay men would never want us, nor we them, so what could it matter what or whom they pursued? "Still, I'm tired of seeing them so damn smug and happy when I haven't met a decent man in three months," my friend, the secretary of the Irates, complained.

"Why do you assume they're happy?" Donald, the one gay member of the Irates, would counter. Donald sought Mr. Right more avidly than we did and argued for the universality of mute telephones and the kind of loneliness that wakes you up at three in the morning. He made sense, but it didn't matter: gay men not only appeared to have an unlimited romantic field to plow, but they invariably shared two high incomes and lived the good life. "When a civil engineer 'marries' an investment advisor and they have no children, you can be sure they don't dine on meat loaf," sighed our secretary.

After eighteen months of membership, I met Mario and resigned from the Irate Celibates. Mated and pleased, my homophobia subsided; it became a nonissue. Looking for the Perfect Apartment, Mario and I actually found it: a deck overlooking a panoramic view of the city, a working fireplace and easy parking. We signed our lease with haste and glee, eager to embark on this urban honeymoon. An identical apartment connected with ours. Its tenants were also a honeymooning couple, Nathan and Luke. Good neighbors, we rang their doorbell, introduced ourselves and suggested we all share our bottle of wine. Also good neighbors, they led us on a tour of their apartment. Identical in layout to ours, Nathan and Luke had created an unabashed decorating vision of white plush couches, exotic flowering plants and track lighting. Or at least Nathan had. Older and calmer, Nathan was obviously the domestic force. He fetched the crystal for our toast to New Neighbors; undoubtedly he'd be washing it when we left. Luke was blond and ebullient; he gave us an entertaining five-minute rundown on the neighborhood at large. Mario and I liked them both.

"I feel like Harriet Nelson," Mario complained, once back in our abode of the beige carpet and the standing lamps. Mario, the more visually astute between us, was in charge of home aesthetics. Talented though he was, he was domestically surpassed by Nathan. "Never mind," I said. "It may look great, but there wasn't one piece of reading material in their entire apartment."

"Are you going to lecture on how juvenile crime rates would go down if all junior high students were forced to read *Crime and Punishment*?" Mario knew well my aspirations to literary snobbery. "Besides, there was an *Architectural Digest* on the coffee table."

"Oh," I said, emphatically unimpressed. If I am a book snob, Mario was a music snob. I awaited his observations of their record collection. "Too much disco," he snorted. Our pompous assessments stopped there; we were approaching dangerous personal ground. I thought music meant Motown and Mario thought *Crime and Punishment* was some sort of legal text. It was best to move on to other topics.

When Indian summer came, our neighbors were often on the deck, tanning their substantial pectoral muscles. Mario complained that he could not take his shirt off in their company because he was too out of shape. "You're gorgeous," I assured him, and he was. "Anyway, you could look like them if you worked out three times a week." That clinched it. Mario retained his shirt and his alabaster tone.

While our deck sported a couple of depressed plants and one of those ubiquitous black-domed barbecues, Nathan and Luke's was a wonderland of potted foliage, more track lighting and a domed barbecue in brilliant red. Still happy in my honeymoon state, these and all other lifestyle discrepancies struck me as merely amusing. I was in that safe cocoon—neither celibate nor irate; I was flourishing. I slowly got to know Nathan and Luke. As my cocoon shedded some of its secure furry substance, I got to know them better yet.

=====

When tanning weather ended, only Luke and I ventured onto the deck, usually clad in bathrobes, on difficult marital mornings. Elbows on our respective railings, we'd survey the cityscape before us and whine. "Nathan's always on my case," Luke would say, running a hand through his blond curls. "He thinks I have too much fun." I'd sip my tea and say, "I'm not too fond of Mario today either." Luke and I fancied ourselves to be Lucy Ricardo derivatives: well-meaning but errant housewives to be chastised when the stern Ricky got home. We were naughty, irresponsible grasshoppers, ever suppressed by our industrious ant counterparts. So maligned! Schizophrenically, I would later adopt the ant viewpoint while discussing with Nathan the importance of The Home.

I often wished we could give each other marital tips. Were straight and gay marriages salvaged with the same techniques? I thought of Barbara, a dear friend forty years of age. She switched sexual allegiances at thirty, after a ten-year marriage. "The best thing about being gay," she had told me, "is that when I'm angry with Sharon, I'm angry with her on a personal basis only. With my husband, it was personal *and* political anger. Sharon and I don't have to fight the gender war." Ah yes, the ancient battle of the sexes. Without this tedious legacy, I wondered just what battleground Luke and Nathan did fight on?

I had my chance to examine said battleground a few nights later. Mario and I had just had one of our stupider fights: "Why Do We Split the Bills in Half When Mario Makes Twice My Salary?" He had left the house for a while; I was steaming on the couch. The moon was in Divorce Court that night, for two anguished voices came wafting through the wall, punctuated by the infernal disco beat. It had to be severe; we could rarely hear them. I was tired of my despair and I wanted to hear someone else's— a self-conscious voyeur, I put my ear to the wall. Hideously, I heard Mario and myself in the guise of Nathan and Luke.

"You have to try," Nathan was wailing. "Relationships don't work unless you try." His voice alternately faded and grew; he was pacing the floor. I had often said those very words in my Camille stance, draped across furniture, beaten down. I could hear Luke washing the dishes. He was not speaking. Why were these scenes always blocked the same way? Camille languishes and sobs; the adversary stiffly performs some inane household chore to infuriate Camille still further. Having performed both roles to perfection, I couldn't begin to guess where my sympathies lay. I pried myself from the wall, glad that Mario hadn't witnessed this indulgence. I could certainly never reveal such a trespass to Luke or Nathan.

Preoccupied with other things (none of which were me), Mario missed out on the neighbors' friendship. He didn't cultivate them. I courted them individually and occasionally together. While Luke monopolized their deck, the front yard was Nathan's territory. Pulling weeds together, we too discussed our domestic situations—the ant's vision.

"Luke is the kind of person who likes to eat a burrito on the run," Nathan would say. "I like candlelight dinners at home. It's a drag to cook for someone who doesn't appreciate it." Nathan was the protector of home and hearth, and I knew what he meant. I loved presenting a leg of lamb surrounded by fresh mint and baby artichokes, then basking in Mario's approval. Unfortunately, Mario was spending too much time at work to approve of such endeavors. Maybe I should cook for Nathan? Or he for me? Should Luke and Mario be eating burritos on the run together?

I was still receiving Irate Celibates newsletters; the unlucky Donald was still a member. We met over coffee where I described my neighbors. "They're terrific. I'm lucky to have them."

"Gay men don't make you cranky any more?" he asked suspiciously.

Although my honeymoon glow was well dimmed by that point, I had to admit that I no longer blamed heterosexual failings on the gay community.

"We have a new division in the Irates now," Donald confided. "It's called 'Wayward Celibates.' That means you can have a disappointing romantic encounter and still be welcomed back to the fold." We laughed uproariously. Although I didn't miss celibacy, I did miss this type of banter: humor as a balm. Mario was somber, increasingly so.

By the time Indian Summer came around again, Nathan and Luke's chests were resplendent with muscles and Mario and I were in couple therapy. I conferred with Luke on the deck; I conferred with Nathan in the front yard; I conferred with myself while driving to work in tears. Futility reigned. Mario and his stereo departed after six counseling sessions; I was left with my books. I knew Nathan and Luke had watched him leave, and an hour later they rang my bell with a bottle of champagne in hand.

"We know this isn't a particularly happy time," said Luke, "but certain rituals in life must be observed." Of course he was right. I felt like I was at my own funeral, and one always drank and ate copious amounts after a funeral. "Sit down," I said. "I'll get the glasses." We had met over a ceremonious drink; we were having one again.

"What shall we drink to?" asked Nathan, while Luke poured this celebratory spirit. I could see that this was up to me. I pondered, fighting tears.

"How about the finding of love, the keeping of love and perhaps a little dignity along the way?"

They smiled and lifted their glasses high. I knew Luke was struggling with the keeping of love, and certainly Nathan wanted the dignity he felt he deserved. We finished the bottle.

Donald called the next week to ask if I'd be rejoining the Irates. As a former member, my entrance fee would be waived.

"I don't think I qualify just now," I told him. "I'm not irate." This was true: I was sad and unquestionably celibate, but the fury had gone out of me. I wanted to rest. "Let's have lunch and put the club on the back burner for now."

21. Single Angst

The first thing that happened the day my boyfriend Hank moved out was the group suicide of my bathroom towel racks. The moment they figured out I was living alone, they unscrewed themselves from the wall and jumped, like eager lemmings, to the tile floor. "This is a test of self-reliance!" they taunted me as they fell. "Go get a screwdriver!"

"I'm flunking the test and I don't care!" I taunted back, hanging my towels neatly over the shower rod.

The next night all the lightbulbs situated four feet over my head burned out. "Stand on a chair, remove these dead-bug–infested fixtures, and replace us!" they screamed.

"Overhead lighting is unaesthetic!" I screamed back, flicking on a floor lamp. Should I fall off a chair and split my skull open? Should I electrocute myself?

I'd read in women's magazines that I should learn to perform these tasks myself, but I refused. I am not one to unjam Xerox machines. I am the kind of woman who drives right past self-serve on to the Princess pumps. Newly single, I was having enough gender identification trouble without doing the chores that males were surely designed to do. My diminished self-image craved a parasol and a mint julep on the veranda, not a monkey wrench and a beer.

=====

The fates disapproved; the conspiracy continued. Doorknobs leapt off doors; faucets sprang leaks; pictures begged to be hung on the wall. "Fiddle-dee-dee," I tittered, giving my invisible parasol a nonchalant twirl. When my bed frame collapsed, I stopped twirling. I needed help. I decided to call Phil, with whom I'd shared an uncomplicated friendship since college. Since Alice had left him, Phil was emphatically single. I knew he owned a tool kit, and I also happened to know he ate canned chili five nights a week.

"Phil, I'll cook a wonderful dinner if you come over and pretend to be my husband," I said.

"Isn't that a little callous? Who am I—Stan Stud? And anyway, didn't we decide seven years ago that sex wasn't in our mutual scenario?"

"No, Phil. I need you to be Mr. Fix-It. Sort of my handyman, but not that kind."

"Oh." A pause. "Can we have rack of lamb?"

I'd been dining on Lean Cuisine and wine since my breakup, so Phil's lamb feast prompted my first real trip to the supermarket. I was overwhelmed by its size, scope, and cruelly infinite selection. Living alone, what should one buy and why? I knew my crisper would fill with rotting produce, that huge loaves of bread would be barely penetrated before going stale. Perversity struck; my impulse was to shoplift a frozen pizza and flee. But Phil needed to be bribed.

Resigned, I selected a cart and pushed it down two aisles before realizing it had been designed by Stephen King. Had Mr. King designed all the carts? I looked around. No—only mine. It propelled itself straight to the diet root beer, one of Hank's more disgusting staples.

"No!" I hissed, overpowering it and steering it to the dairy case, halting before the cheese. Reaching for Danish Havarti, I stood aghast as eight ounces of smoked Gouda jumped into the cart.

"He liked smoked Gouda, not I!" I yelped, tossing it back like a tiny fish. People stared. I hastily abandoned the demonic cart and gathered my groceries in my arms, Phil's rack of lamb bleeding only slightly on my coat sleeve. Single life was horrifying.

I unpacked my groceries in the kitchen, on friendly turf at last. Food was glorious; it did not require screwdrivers. I coated the lamb with bread crumbs, mustard, and garlic and slid it into the oven. The asparagus stood in its steamer, ready for action. I was Woman.

And Phil was Man—a slightly chubby one I noticed, when I opened the door. Too much canned chili. He was dressed in jeans, a T-shirt, and a tool kit. Calm befell me. My house would be tamed.

"I can smell the lamb," he said appreciatively. "This will be my first real meal in weeks. Do you have any Scotch?"

I looked to see if Hank had forgotten the Glenlivet I'd given him last Christmas; luckily he had. I made two large drinks. Phil headed for the bathroom and set his glass on the edge of the tub. I followed him and watched as he magically remounted the towel racks.

"It's mystical," I said.

"It's easy," he said.

I offered him a footstool to change the lights, but he was tall enough to do it alone. I handed him the new bulbs, announcing, "It's mystical!" with each new illumination.

"Can I have another drink?" he asked. He followed me into the kitchen. "Are you okay?" he added. "Why do you suddenly think everything's mystical?"

I tried to explain about being alone and having my house hate me, and hating it back, and not being able to do masculine chores and wanting to be Princess Parasol forever, and about the Stephen

King shopping cart. "Everything's falling apart," I finished, breathlessly. I made myself another drink and freshened his.

"No, everything just seems like it's falling apart," he said.

"That's close enough for me." I turned the heat on under the steamer. "Do you still like hollandaise on your asparagus?"

Phil's eyes glowed. "Alice used to make that. I loved it. Can I watch?" He stood behind me and studied carefully while I separated two eggs, letting the whites slip and slide down the drain.

"It's mystical," he said. "Women can do such mystical things." He looked at me as if I held the key to the universe. "I took a cooking class after Alice and I split up," he confessed as I whisked the yolks into melted butter. "But I think I was too depressed to learn. I kept burning everything—the food, my hands, the potholders. And I always sliced my finger with the paring knife. I hate meals."

"That's because you eat canned chili."

"That's exactly right."

"Do you like your lamb pink?"

"It's more mystical pink," he said.

As if we weren't drunk enough on Hank's Glenlivet, I brought out a bottle of Cabernet Sauvignon and handed Phil the corkscrew.

"You can't open wine?" he asked.

"That's a man corkscrew," I explained. "I had a woman corkscrew but I guess Hank took it." The woman corkscrew was easy to use; the man wasn't. That was the formula.

Phil opened and poured the wine. He held my glass to my lips so I could taste it while pouring hollandaise on the asparagus. "Mystical wine," he said.

"Mystical," I agreed. He ate everything I served him, telling me how amazing the dinner was and how happy it made him. I was glad he'd failed his cooking class. The more wine I drank, the more competent his biceps looked. He could probably put a new roof on my house if he wanted to.

"My bed collapsed!" I suddenly remembered.

"Let's go fix it," he said, carrying the glasses and the rest of the wine to my bedroom. "Things *are* falling apart," he said, surveying the mess of boards and rumpled sheets.

"No, they only seem like they are," I corrected him. And, like Hercules or Atlas, he hammered nails until I had a bed frame again. I couldn't believe it. He just kept knowing what to do.

I smoothed the sheet over the mattress, and my down quilt over that.

"Let's test it," Phil urged, bouncing on the bed to see if it would hold.

"Okay," I agreed, not sure what I was agreeing to. Drunk and exhilarated, I joined him on the bed. We bounced.

"Mystical, isn't it?" he asked, pushing me gently downward.

"Incredibly so," I said. Phil's face doubled in size because he was kissing me. Then, as I tried to synthesize the opposing concepts of Phil and sex, the bed collapsed again. I *knew* Phil had been eating too much chili. Boards, nails, and pillows flew around the room, splattered with Cabernet. I silently thanked God.

Phil lay quietly for about a minute. "Are we embarrassed?" he asked.

I lay across his legs, hoping the ceiling wouldn't start to spin. "Well, we're embarrassed, but not as embarrassed as we might have been," I said.

Neither of us moved.

"I wanted to make love to you because you cooked dinner," he said, sounding awed.

"But sex isn't part of our mutual scenario, remember?"

"I know. But the hollandaise really got to me. I must be going crazy."

"Maybe you miss Alice."

"Nah, just her hollandaise."

I shook my legs out a little, wondering if I could stand up. Phil grabbed one of them.

"Tell me something," he said. "Did you entertain the thought, or think maybe it would be nice, I mean just for a minute . . . you know?"

"Phil," I said, "I'm crazier than you are. I was ready to *marry* you because you put up my towel racks."

He guffawed. It was very loud. Then he said, "I'm too drunk to fix your bed again. Do you have any dessert?"

I did. Chocolate Decadence waited in the refrigerator, so we ate it and tried to sober up with coffee. Phil raved about it, but in a purely friendly way. We were relaxed; more to the point, we were relieved.

"I guess I'll sleep on the couch tonight," I said.

"I'll come over tomorrow and fix your bed," he offered.

"Do you think I'm incompetent for not learning to do it myself?"

"No, I'm glad you won't learn. It makes me feel like Mr. Macho."

"Good. Then I'll make breakfast for us tomorrow. It makes me feel less asexual."

We said good night, and I went to brush my teeth. I gave my towel racks a playful tug; mystically, they stayed intact. Mystically, I thought, so might I.

22. Death of a Duck

Peter and I enjoyed a most exquisite sense of play in our love affair; I miss it more than anything else. Since he's gone, my psychic playground has shut down. The swing set is empty; the slide deserted. Whimsy has died on the vine and its death leaves me old and brittle. I live again in the adult world—literal and dry.

He deemed me a duck early on, spontaneously over dinner. "You look just like a duck! Seriously, you do," he observed one night. It's true enough: My lips are ungenerous, which gives me a duck bill, and my hips are decidedly womanly as are those of ducks. "Duckie!" he said, triumphantly, refilling our wineglasses. "You are my own sweet duck, my adored feathered friend!"

I was delighted to be a duck, and I was, over three years' time, every possible kind of duck. Peter became one too by virtue of proximity, and we both began to quack. We quacked only in private for a long time, experimenting with this new form of speech. We learned that fatigue is no reason not to communicate; one can always muster up a quiet quack or two. The style of quacks was many and varied: the resigned quack, the adamant quack, the inquisitive quack and even the quack of stirring lust.

Those who have not quacked can never comprehend its soothing effect; we were increasingly amazed at the power of this balm. Peter sang bilingual songs to me in the morning, just after the alarm emitted its annoying quack. He sang improvisationally and without melody, in both English and Duck:

> "We're in the pond,
> We're in the nest,
> Duckie's the duck
> I love the best!
> Quack, quack, quack!"

He'd quack on into the shower. Lying in bed I could hear the rest of the song under the rush of water. It made me feel unspeakably safe, not knowing yet how unspeakable the illusion of safety is.

The metaphor expanded. Our house was the pond, our bed the nest. "Let's read the paper in the nest," Peter would suggest on many Sunday mornings. We'd gather our preferred sections of the newspaper and our steaming cups of English breakfast tea, and settle in among pillows and comforters. "I wish the pond were insulated," I'd complain in the winter when temperatures plunged.

Duck artifacts began appearing throughout the pond: framed pictures of ducks, plates and bowls with ducks painted on them, ducky dish towels. One night Peter brought home the ultimate duck: She was a huge ceramic peasant, a duck of Slavic origin like myself, wearing a big blue babushka that tied beneath her chin. She stood on my grandmother's Russian tea cart, a testament to our mutual heritage. Her bill was parted in continual silent speech, her orange webbed feet planted solidly on her Ukrainian turf. We presided, in tandem, over the kitchen. Her first night home she watched us dine on roast chicken. "A distant relative?" asked Peter, taking carving knife to bird. "Very distant," I assured him, feeling the Slavic duck's black eyes upon my back.

It occurred to me that not all couples operated in this fashion.

"What do you call Michael?" I asked my friend Lisa, never having heard mention of a nickname.

"Michael," she told me.

Oh. I had at least seven names (and variations on these) for Peter, and he for me. We'd recite them like mantras, as we did all our inane question-and-answer routines:

"Who's cute?"

"You."

"No, who is really cute?"

"You."

"No, who is so gorgeous that it boggles the mind?"

"All right," a sheepish smile. "I guess it's me."

Every night when Peter came home from work, he'd greet me with a raucous quack. I would be in the kitchen, preparing dinner with the help of the Slavic duck. Occasionally I'd have a friend with me, whom Peter could not immediately see. "Is your boyfriend crazy?" read the look on the friend's face. Peter was only briefly embarrassed by this exposure; then all self-consciousness vanished. After all, the way of the duck was a good way. "Come, Duckie, come crawl under my wing," he'd say to me when I was unhappy. "Let me smooth those ruffled feathers. Let me kiss your bill."

Bypassing measles and nightmares, we had stolen back the richest gems of childhood: the art of fantasy and play. It was innocence itself, proven repeatedly by the fact that when we argued, no quacks sounded. Duck talk was for love and levity. We reserved the evolved language of humans for arguments and pain.

Although ducks could not be angry, they certainly could be sad. Peter and I excelled in metaphor, but failed in reality. He vacated the pond, leaving me alone with the Sunday paper in our queen-size nest. But it wasn't a nest any more, it was merely a bed. And I, after a thousand days and nights of quacking, was no longer a duck. His disappearance broke the spell. I reverted to human form as predictably as in any Grimms' fairy tale. Gone were the magic and the illusion of safety.

I gave away the ducky dish towels and hid the framed duck pictures in the garage. Though I tried to avert my eye from the Russian tea cart, I could still feel the Slavic duck's reproachful glance. Never try to fool a duck wearing a babushka. She knew she had to be dealt with.

First comes the death of content; then one must kill the symbols. Lady Macbeth had nothing on me the night I finally carried my ceramic duck to the garbage can, placing her gently between stacks of newspapers. Her black beady eyes were the last thing I saw before replacing the cold, gray lid. Lying awake at five that morning, I could hear the garbage men come to take her away. I've buried her alive, I thought. But there was nothing else to do, nothing else to do.

My heart is broken for myriad reasons, but I think the most powerful one is the death of play. How can I quack now? Who would understand it? I have to hope that I will be loved again. My fear is that I will not be nicknamed.

Alone

23. It Makes You Want to Shout

ast Saturday night I wanted to go out dancing. I craved loud rock and roll and a frenetic, forgetting evening. And last Saturday night, as on a long string of Saturday nights before it, I noted that all my friends were currently involved in some type of domestic state. They were spending their weekends performing the serene rituals that make most of us want to be mated: cooking pasta for two, watching rented films on their VCRs. This meant that if I wanted to go dancing, I'd have to go by myself.

It's annoying and inconvenient to be in a different romantic cycle from one's friends. If you're single and they're not, they'll only see you for lunch. I was the same way when I was cooking pasta for two; timing is everything, and it can't be helped. So why, I asked myself, should I stay home with all this dance energy inside me just because I didn't have a date or a female companion? Would this keep a man home? Besides, I had a car, and this was more essential than company.

While I put on a T-shirt, jeans, contact lenses and shoes that wouldn't slip off, I wondered how stupid I'd feel walking into the dance club alone. Then I remembered my own theory of Universal Anonymity: no one ever pays attention to what anyone else is doing, so why feel stupid about anything? This gave me courage, and I drove full speed ahead to Haight Street, parking just a block from the club.

I chose this particular night spot for two reasons: it plays music from the fifties and sixties, and it is decidedly Not Slick. The clientele is eclectic; welders and plumbers abound, as do attorneys, although you can't tell by looking at them. You can be fat, you can be an aging hippie still pungent with patchouli oil, you can commit major fashion errors, and no one notices. It's relaxing.

I locked my purse and coat in the trunk, so that neither would be stolen or drenched in beer, and ran through the cold to the entrance. I was equipped with only my keys, a lipstick, a five-dollar bill and the phrase "my girlfriend's parking the car," in case anyone happened to ask.

"Got some ID?" the doorman asked me, grinning. I'm thirty-four and he was pushing forty. I asked him if he was serious; he wasn't. He waved me into a sea of peers—scores of men and women in their thirties, drinking and dancing against an adolescent backdrop. I ordered a beer, resisting the urge to order a second one for my invisible companion, and listened to the Marvelettes sing "Please, Mr. Postman."

A huge, brightly lit jukebox dominated the room, housing the teen years of everybody in the place. When it let forth with "He's So Fine," I could see pixie bands emerging from all the women's hairlines, and I smelled English Leather and Jade East wafting up from the men's faces. This kind of music takes you right back to junior high with an amazing force: suddenly, ages are halved, and imported beer starts to taste like warm rum and Coke in a paper cup. When Johnny Mathis comes on, you think you're back in a suburban rumpus room, dreaming about marriage. Of course, by now all these dancers had been married and divorced, battered and shattered, but were resilient as hell.

If hearing the Isley Brothers sing parts one and two of "Shout!" doesn't cure your adult depression, I can only recommend serious drug therapy. Meanwhile, my beer was cold, perfect. I was glad to be exactly where I was. I was standing alone but, unlike my junior-high-school self, I was hoping no one would ask me to dance. I had sympathy for the would-be aggressor—it's horrible to ask someone to dance and be refused—but I wanted to choose my own partner. I like to stand for a while and assess the dance skills of the men on the floor. If I see someone who's really energetic and fairly competent, I wait to see if he has a date for the evening. If he doesn't, I assume a confident air and ask him to dance. I don't worry excessively about being turned down; I suspect that men will dance with anyone at least once. They know they can always get away.

=====

All the good dancers seemed to be with steady partners, so I took a break and wandered past the video games. Wandering back, I saw three drunk boys weaving by the monolithic jukebox.

"Wanna dance?" their spokesman asked me. Groups of males always have a spokesman.

They were young, cute, nonthreatening. "Which of you is the best dancer?" I asked. I could see who was the best looking—the spokesman—but that wasn't my concern.

The two taller ones immediately pointed to the stalky blond in the middle. "Bobby!" they exclaimed. "No doubt about it. Bobby dances."

Bobby was about my height and was decked out in some bizarre but oddly attractive outfit of high-waisted pants, white suspenders and a purple shirt, all fitted smoothly over his tight, sturdy body. His hair was blond and layered, ending in what looked like a half-formed braid in the back. I didn't understand this fashion; maybe, I thought, it has something to do with youth.

"You can dance?" I asked him, directly.

"Try me," he challenged, leading me out to the center of the room. We staked out our dance territory of two square feet, and within a couple of minutes we'd circled the floor three times. I nodded approvingly.

"No kidding—you're a great dancer," I said. He really was. Even though he was drunk, he was quite serious about doing a good job; he took pride in the art form. He understood economy of movement and space; when I moved too far from him, he'd draw me back with a firm ease, never missing a beat. His motion was clean and fluid. He made me feel like Ginger Rogers.

"Where'd you learn to dance so well?" I asked him at the end of "Tighten Up." Being well-danced is—well, it's right up there.

"My roommates and I practice at home. Like, we buy a keg of beer, put on the old records and dance the night away."

"You mean guys?"

"Yeah. We go to Chico State. We're here for a wedding. That's why we're so ripped—been drinking champagne all afternoon."

Oh God—college. I didn't have the nerve to ask him what his major was. "So why do you dance with your roommates? Don't you know any women? I mean, girls?" Maybe this explained the braid.

"Yeah, we go out and dance with girls, but sometimes it's too much trouble. It's just as fun with my roommates." "Baby Love" came on the jukebox, and Bobby took my hands in his, diligently counting out the beats in the introduction before launching me into a spin. "Anyway," he continued earnestly when I returned from spinning, "lots of girls won't do touch dancing. I take their hands and they back off, saying they don't *do* that. That's why I like dancing with you—you're into the steps."

It was hard to answer during "Baby Love." I waited till Ms. Ross faded out and said, "I grew up with this kind of dancing. That's why I like it."

He looked at me closely. "How old are you?"

"Thirty-four."

Bobby started to giggle. He wiped his brow with one sturdy arm. "You don't look it."

"The hell I don't. You just don't know what thirty-four looks like. How old are you?"

"Christ. Nineteen."

"How'd you get in here?"

"Fake ID."

We danced another dance, and like everything else that's well practiced, it got better and better. "Get ready for a double twirl," Bobby would warn me. Prepared, I would execute the step without skidding into the wall. By the next dance, I didn't even need the warning.

"Hey, all right!" Bobby shouted, preening. "We're getting good! Let's reward ourselves with a beer." He pushed me toward the bar and bought two Buds. "Hey, do you mind if we just dance together the rest of the night? I mean, I don't see much point in changing partners when it's working out."

My sentiments exactly. When I find a good partner, I stick like glue, even if he is nineteen. "I'm not going anywhere," I promised him, as "Shout!" started playing. The whole room went crazy, especially Bobby, his little body newly pumped with Isley Brothers adrenalin. He must have been inspired by the toga party in *Animal House*. We abandoned our beers and headed back to the floor. "I love this part!" Bobby yelled when they sang "Now waaaaaaaaaiiiiiit a minute!" between sides one and two.

Clearly, he knew every word to every hit made before he was even born. I'd calculated: he was born in 1965, the year *Rubber Soul* came out.

"Bobby, shouldn't you be listening to the Police or something? Why do you like oldies so much?"

No one could have looked more indignant than this boy in white suspenders: "It's not my fault I was born too late. This music's the best."

$=$

"Sealed with a Kiss" was playing, and Bobby and I adjusted ourselves for a slow dance. He was very gentlemanly about it, making no untoward moves. Then he whispered in my ear, "You're not *really* thirty-four, are you?"

"Yeah, I really, really am," I said. I figured that Bobby's parents were in their forties, his friends were all nineteen, and I was the only person in my age group that he'd ever actually met.

"Are you married or what?" he asked next.

"I guess I'm what."

"Nice earrings," he complimented me.

"Nice suspenders," I returned. I stood back and looked at him a minute. "Is this how the youth of today is dressing?" I was trying to work up courage to ask him about the braid.

"Hey, this is how *Bobby Benton* dresses," he said, pulling himself up to full height. "I don't *know* about the youth of today." He's so cocky, I thought. It's wonderful. We continued dancing.

"So what are you doing later on?" he asked.

"Going home and going to sleep." I was looking forward to it. I'd used every muscle in my body; I felt better than I ever did after an aerobics class.

"So why don't you take me with you?"

I almost laughed, but checked myself. "Because I don't want to." Was that unkind? "I mean, it's not appropriate."

"Why not?"

"Because I didn't come here for that. I came to dance."

He started nuzzling my ear, just like in junior high. "You should take me home, you know," he wheedled, nearly disengaging my earring with his teeth. Fortunately, they were clip-ons.

"Why should I?"

"Because I'm young. I'm strong. You *know* I can dance. I'm good."

I was amazed; he was actually trying to talk me into it. Listing his assets. A sales pitch. I gave myself over to erotic thought for fifteen seconds. Who knows: the nineteen-year-old Bobby Benton might be the catalyst for myriad sexual revelations; he might be a better cure for depression than the Isley Brothers.

Right. I pictured myself donning a frilled apron, cooking his breakfast to teenage specification and driving him to a bus stop so he could get back to Chico. I'd probably have to reconstruct his braid for him. He'd probably try to get me to iron his high-waisted pants.

"Bobby, you're cute and sweet and a terrific dancer, but I'm going home alone," I said. I looked at my watch; it was one-thirty. "And I'd better go."

"I'll walk you out," he said. Mrs. Benton had taught her son some etiquette, anyway. We walked past his two friends, who were now three times drunker than when they came in, and past the video games to the doorway. It was cold outside.

"My coat's in the car," I said. "I've got to run for it."

"You can wear mine," he offered.

"You don't have one."

"Oh, yeah." He looked sheepish, then cocky again. "Are you *sure* you don't want to take me to your apartment? You don't have roommates, do you?"

I was getting impatient. "Bobby, no one my age has roommates." I looked out at Haight Street. In 1967, the Summer of Love, I was seventeen and Bobby was two. Maybe not even toilet trained. I refrained from vocalizing this observation. "If you come here again, I'd *love* to dance with you. Call me," I said, writing down my number on the inevitable paper napkin. "Seriously—you're the best dancer I've ever known."

"That's why you should take me home!" he whined. Ah, the sexual urgency of the nineteen-year-old body. It was pure, basic, even flattering, but not nearly enough.

"Good night," I said, and walked briskly to my car. It was freezing; I retrieved my purse, put on my coat and started the motor. Checking my watch again, I saw I'd danced with Bobby for four hours straight. My arms ached a little as I steered my way out of the tight parking space. A hot shower before bed would feel good. Then tomorrow I'd make breakfast for one and think about Bobby Benton in Chico. I would have to remember to ask someone about that braid.

24. Resurrection Omelet

"Never trust a man who won't eat eggs," Sally's mother tells us as I set her resurrection omelet before her. Sally rolls her eyes and reaches for the raspberry preserves. She has heard her mother's treatises on men and eggs before: the tricks of careful coddling, the avoidance of the overly hardboiled. I have heard them, too, but Mrs. West is not my mother and so her excesses do not upset me.

My resurrection omelet is exactly that; lightly beaten eggs folded in butter and strewn with chopped parsley, the greenery a testament to spring. I have eaten it every Easter Sunday for years.

"The egg is nature's masterpiece," Mrs. West continues. She is seventy years old and still beautiful. "The perfect self-contained structure. Strong, yet fragile. And there is no yellow more vivid than that of a fresh yolk."

I think well of these life ovals, too. "I like their flexibility," I say. "They're altered forever with a hint of heat or the flick of a wrist."

Mrs. West cuts into her eggs and pats my hand. She possesses good bones and blue eyes the color of robin's eggs. Eros has gently dictated her life; Sally, who did not inherit her mother's beauty, has followed the lead of pragmatism. I suspect that Sally must look like her father, the third of Mrs. West's four husbands. He died when Sally was seven. Mrs. West divorced the other three.

"Thank you for having me over," Mrs. West says to me. "I needed a resurrection this morning. Marjorie and I—well, truthfully, just I—had a small setback yesterday."

Marjorie has been a widow for five years and Mrs. West's close friend for fifty. I pour out more Darjeeling tea and ask what this setback might be.

"Yesterday," she begins, "was one of those glorious days full of sunshine and possibility. Marjorie and I were both dressed in new frocks."

"Frock?" Sally frowns. "No one over twelve wears a frock." The mother-daughter edge; it's as eternal as the egg.

"Spring dresses, then. Hers was yellow, mine blue. My dress exactly matched my eyes." I am alternately annoyed with Mrs. West's vanity and encouraged by it.

"We took the bus to Union Street to visit Lucy. You remember Lucy, don't you?" She looks at Sally. "The three of us went to school together a thousand years ago." Mrs. West uses hyperbole when she is uncomfortable. It is easier for her to recall college as a millennium past, rather than the half century it is.

"Yes, Lucy's the one who stayed married."

"Right. To Henry, the most boring man in California."

"Of his generation," I clarify. "We both know contenders for that title." Sally and I enjoy a running debate on which man we know is the more maniacally boring: Michael Herbert, who talks about tax shelters, or Joe Simon, who discusses stock options. Both inspire instant narcolepsy.

"Henry had a stroke. He's in a wheelchair."

"I'm sorry," Sally hastens. "We didn't mean . . . "

"Don't be stupid, dear. He was boring before the stroke and now he is more boring. Only now he has justification. My point is that Lucy has to care for him around the clock. It's made her old."

"She's seventy, Mom."

"I didn't say it made her seventy; I said it made her old."

"Do you mean she wasn't wearing a frock?"

"That's precisely what I mean." Mrs. West has told Sally and me many times that the psyche never ages. It's a warning, I think, but I can't quite define what she is warning us against. "The moment we walked into their dark apartment we lost our buoyant mood. Lucy was wearing a housedress, even though she was expecting us. And slippers. Our dresses and hats were an affront to her. And she'd gotten fat."

"Some of us do get fat," Sally reminds her. Mrs. West is spreading more butter on her blueberry muffin. Along with her exquisite face, she is blessed with a perfectly formed body. She has never taken care of it, and it has never betrayed her. Marjorie told Sally once that when their crowd was in their frivolous twenties, Mrs. West would show up at parties with damp, newly washed hair and no makeup and still look better than any woman there. "It was infuriating," she said, needlessly.

===

Mrs. West eats her muffin thoughtfully and asks for more orange juice. I pour it all around, weighing its vibrant color against that of an egg yolk. The egg, I decide, is still nature's superior child. From it comes everything.

"The three of us sat down in Lucy's kitchen and drank tea. From tea bags, mind you," she says, nodding approval at the loose tea leaves settled at the bottom of my blue Wedgwood teapot. Mrs. West taught me to read tea leaves years ago, but I cannot do it now.

"And over the tea, we began to catch up. Marjorie and I did all the talking, and we didn't discuss the past—only the present. We told Lucy what we're up to now." Mrs. West used to act in amateur theater groups; Sally claims she quit when they started offering her parts for older women. Now she organizes theater parties; groups of friends attend a play and critique it afterward over a potluck dinner. Marjorie goes to city planning meetings and works on political campaigns. These are busy women.

"Lucy listened silently to our stories, one eye on Henry, who was stationed in the living room with an army blanket over his knees. We finally ran out of things to say and sat listening to Lucy's teaspoon tapping against her cup. I began to feel terribly sorry for her, for her white hair, for her sad little dress, for her burdens. I was going to ask her to come out with us, for a walk in the park to see the roses."

"My mother has received more roses from men than anyone I know," Sally told me once. "But I don't think she's ever sent them."

"I was about to speak when Lucy looked at me and decided to break her silence. It was the strangest thing," she says, studying a parsley sprig as she twirls it slowly between thumb and forefinger.

"What did she say?" I ask.

"She said: 'I slept with Robert in 1945.' "

Robert was Mrs. West's second husband, the black-haired, handsome one she met in the theater. He not only disliked eggs, he was allergic to them. Forsaking eggs for the duration of their marriage, Mrs. West had learned to perfect potato pancakes, his preferred breakfast.

"Lucy and Robert?" Sally is incredulous. "Forty years ago? That bastard." She never liked him or any of her mother's husbands, except for her own father.

"Yes, Robert was a bastard. I couldn't agree more," Mrs. West responds. Robert has been dead for ten years, a victim of a heart attack, despite his eggless existence. Mrs. West still scrutinizes her sprig of parsley because she does not want to look at us. I begin clearing the dishes.

"I can't believe Lucy would betray Henry," Sally mumbles.

"Do you think your generation invented infidelity?" Mrs. West asks. This seems to me an unkind question; Sally's own marriage was destroyed by her husband's unending sexual conquests. "It's because I'm not pretty," Sally used to agonize. I had told her that as far as I could tell, infidelity had far more to do with the betrayer than the one betrayed.

"Then I can't believe that Robert would betray you," Sally answers. They say you can salvage a curdled hollandaise sauce by adding two tablespoons of boiling water and beating it like mad. It's never worked for anyone I know, though; the sauce always has to be thrown out.

"I can believe it. I'd just never thought about it."

"But why did she tell you now?" Sally implores. "Why keep a secret like that for forty years and then spring it on you like this?"

"And why in front of Marjorie?" Mrs. West adds. The sin of humiliation is lain neatly atop the sin of sexual betrayal.

I return to the table and see Mrs. West looking her age for the first time. I am astonished by the power—indeed, even the posthumous power—of sexual infidelity. It is such a constant and common phenomenon that it strikes me as hardly worth noting. Yet, of all the infinite varieties of betrayal in the world, the ones that earn the most attention all seem to be sexual in nature. No one is immune; beauty is no protection. I imagine the deafening crack that must have resounded when Humpty Dumpty fell from his wall.

"Maybe she made it up," I blurt. Sally looks at me gratefully; Mrs. West lets her parsley sprig fall to the soiled tablecloth.

"That occurred to me," says Mrs. West, smiling in a rather mean way. "But Lucy's clever. She knows I'll never know."

Even if there were a king to call upon, I suspect that his horses and men would still be incapable of resurrecting the shattered. It's like the hollandaise; perhaps it is arrogant to even try to repair certain damages. I've always felt bad about Sally and her mother's divorces. I've never been through a divorce, but I think that's only because I've never been married.

"Julia Child can crack open an egg in one hand," I say, because no one else is speaking. "Can either of you teach me to do that?"

25. Sex and Myopia

I think I upset my optometrist when I went in to be fitted for soft contact lenses.

"Have you worn contacts before?" Dr. Shapiro asked me. He's young and good looking.

"Yes, five years ago. For a two-year period."

"Why did you stop?"

"I met my boyfriend."

"Why are you starting again?"

"We broke up."

Said boyfriend had made a wonderful suggestion to me early in our relationship: "Contacts are such a bother—why don't you just wear your glasses?"

"You don't mind having a bespectacled girlfriend?" I'd asked. I knew glasses were neutering. Why else would people intentionally place plastic discs on their eyeballs?

"Sweetie, I'd be proud to walk down the street with you if you had a dog and cane." A moving declaration from a man with 20/20 vision. In love and insane, I let my contacts dry up. Three years later, the affair dried up. Then I made my appointment with Dr. Shapiro.

"You look good in your glasses," Dr. Shapiro offered.

"Thanks," I said, detecting tiny jellyfish afloat on his own brown eyes. "But I notice you're not wearing glasses yourself." It's fun to annoy professionals, especially young, attractive ones.

He bristled only slightly. "I need contacts for my work."

"Dr. Takahashi doesn't." I'd seen Dr. Takahashi the week before to have my prescription updated. "He agrees with me that contacts are a nightmare—the heating, the enzyme cleaning, the tearing, replacing—he says he couldn't be bothered."

"Dr. Takahashi is happily married," he said.

"So?"

"So I'm not and neither are you. Contacts are a dating device. Now read this chart."

While identifying hazy block letters for Dr. Shapiro, I thought back to my first contact lens fitting five years ago. I realized then that Mother Nature did not approve of contact lenses because she offered them so much initial resistance. When Dr. Schultz approached my virgin eye with its first prospective lens, the lid fluttered like a psychotic hummingbird.

"Relax," she'd instructed me, as I stared at her plastic coated fingertip heading for my innocent orb. Relax? Why? Mine was a well-working ancient reflex action, the eye's involuntary protection against an intrusive agent. The body knows what's good for it, and my eyelid kept fluttering with a velocity that would shame Scarlett O'Hara. I was embarrassed, after Dr. Schultz's tenth aborted attempt to touch my eye, that I could not somehow overcome this involuntary impulse. And I was afraid that if I didn't overcome this impulse that I'd be imitating Marilyn Monroe in *How To Marry a Millionaire* the rest of my life— walking into bathroom walls, flirting with parking meters. I willed my eye to relax but it would not. "I'm sorry," I finally said to Dr. Schultz. "My eye refuses to let you near it."

Part of the problem was evident: Dr. Schultz was young, mild-mannered, female, and I wasn't afraid of her. True intimidation was required, so she called in the head of the optometry department, a man in his fifties who was graying at the temples like the proverbial trustworthy airline pilot.

"I am putting this onto your eye," he announced, paralyzing me with authoritative male professionalism. I hate the fact that this tactic worked, but work it did. I'd rather have been blinded than yelled at.

I was astounded at the retraining of those involuntary impulses; my eyes learned to accept contacts as casually as teeth accept dental floss. And what an optical deliverance! Suddenly, without the annoyance of glasses, trees had discernible leaves, the leaves had veins, freeway signs could be read before being passed, and everyone's skin needed help. It was wondrous.

But as wondrous as it was, I knew in my myopic heart that the only true motivation to wear contacts was pure and rampant vanity. Indeed, my newly purchased lenses and cleaning paraphernalia were accompanied by a consumer questionnaire. Asked why I'd traded in glasses for contacts, I wrote down exactly that: "Pure and Rampant Vanity." People claim to do it for peripheral vision, convenience in sports, or simply to free the face from that heavy weight. This last is certainly valid for the extremely shortsighted, whose glasses are so thick as to be truly burdensome. But for most of us—the Mildly Myopic Majority—it's just the urge to be a sex kitten. After all, our glasses are lightweight, Reggie Jackson does fine on the field, and peripheral vision is overrated.

"Why do you think glasses are unsexy?" I asked Dr. Shapiro, as he jotted notes on my medical file.

"They imply age, weakness, and handicap," he said, still jotting.

"And intelligence, right?" I know people think my IQ is raised fifteen points whenever I wear my glasses.

"It so happens that people who read a lot *do* have more eye trouble," he said.

"Even if they read Harlequin romances?" Dr. Shapiro looked irritated, but my point was merely that lots of idiots wear glasses, while many astute people have perfect vision. Yet our culture equates myopia with intelligence, and deem both asexual. I've spent a lot of time trying to crack the code: Only the stupid are sexy? If men don't make passes at girls who wear glasses, does the converse apply? If not, does it mean that stupid women are sexy and that intelligent/myopic men are also sexy? Is this why Marilyn Monroe married Arthur Miller? Why didn't the marriage work out?

Sarah, an acquaintance of mine who happens to be a beautiful and skilled attorney, admits to wearing black-framed glasses in the courtroom. The glass is untreated because she has perfect vision. "I do a better job if I feel like I'm being taken more seriously," she says. Sarah believes the glasses decrease her sexuality and increase her intellectual credibility; thus, they probably do.

I also know a woman with a myopic scalp. She wears her glasses perched on her head, keeping her considerable mane of auburn hair in place. I've never seen her look through her frames; I suspect that, like Sarah's, they hold clear glass. But her message is clear: "I am basically more sexy than bright, but I can be seriously smart at any chosen moment."

I remember when it hit me that contacts are ultimately more annoying than glasses; it was when I realized that the first thing I did every day when I got home was remove them. It was only after this optical liberation that I'd kick off my shoes and read my mail. When I asked fellow lens wearers which they discarded first —shoes or lenses—they confessed to the same priority. It's not that contacts are painful or even uncomfortable. It's only that they are undeniably there.

Once I knew the truth about contacts, I found them to be an interesting barometer of well-being. One Thursday night everyone in our office celebrated a collective pay raise with many drinks. Friday morning four people who I'd never even known to be nearsighted came in wearing their glasses. "Put in contacts with this hangover?" one snarled at me. "My eyes would die."

"Gosh, Nick, your eyes aren't so blue today," I couldn't help observing. Tinted contacts yet. He glared at me through his frames and went to his office. Poor Nick: Superman on Thursday night, a wimpy Clark Kent on Friday morning.

"Dr. Shapiro," I said, while he assembled lens care instructions and insurance information for me, "if glasses are unsexy, why is it that sunglasses, just by virtue of being dark, are not?"

"They aren't corrective aids."

As long as we're not caught correcting a natural imperfection, glasses are forgiveable. To wear photo-gray lenses (the glasses that automatically darken in the sunlight) is to ride a roller coaster of acceptability; outside on a sunny day he's a hunk wearing shades, inside he's Woody Allen. Because the sun won't shine at night, he is exposed as myopic unless he's sly. Sitting in the movie theater with Ms. Right, he furtively slips on his glasses just after the lights go down. Just as furtively, he returns them to their case a moment before the lights go up. "I only need them for movies," he explains, as he strolls nonchalantly into the ladies' room. He who cannot read subtitles without glasses is also incapable of locating the refreshment stand. And he should not be driving Ms. Right home.

"Dr. Shapiro, aside from the handicap business, why else are people ashamed to wear glasses?"

He glanced at his watch. "It's a psychological and physical barrier to intimacy. It's hard to kiss someone wearing glasses."

"But they're easier to remove than contacts."

"Contacts don't need to be removed."

"Eventually they do."

"Have you looked into extended wear?"

"Dr. Shapiro, I'm convinced that extended wear is a myth."

My friend Barbara dates more than any living woman. "I always wear my glasses when I'm with a man I don't particularly want to kiss," she says. "It's less likely to happen—somehow harder to negotiate—when glasses have to be dealt with. On the other hand," she adds, "a man who goes ahead and kisses me without removing my glasses first really earns my respect. It's perverse."

The good and patient doctor handed me my new consumer questionnaire. Somewhat updated, it still asked why I was forsaking glasses for contacts. I pondered a minute.

"How about a fashion tint?" I asked. "Do they come in blue-eyed-blonde yet?"

"They're working on it. Meanwhile, we of the brown eyes may have a shade called 'amber.' It makes you look jaundiced."

"Okay, I'll take them straight," I said. I borrowed his pen and wrote down: The Joys of Peripheral Vision as my reason for buying contacts. God knows I've never seen anything worth noting out of the corner of my eye, but I thought it would be amusing to confuse the optical aid industry. Let them think we all want better vision. Dr. Shapiro and I know better.

26. Frozen Food

Kate met the enormous blond with translucent blue eyes at a party which, before he sat next to her, offered her nothing more than smoked salmon. A little drunk and very affable, he'd crashed the party in the most casual and confident of ways and fell upon her with full attention.

He looked at her without reservation and told her she was beautiful.

"You're very large," she said, recalling male attention and how it could literally light up the night. Kate, who had been separated from her husband for a year, was only sporadically attended to, and spent most of her time attuning her ear to the silence of her house.

The enormous blond, a blustery type of man, walked her to her car and kissed her.

"I haven't kissed anyone since July," she told him, and as this was December, he was impressed. She said it for the value of shock and injustice. "You, unkissed?" she wanted him to think. And he did; she saw that he did.

He called her the next day and she let him come by her apartment to take her out for a drink. Now sober but still jovial, he told her again when she opened the door that she was ravishing. They went to a neighborhood bar where the blond ordered two hot brandies. The second round was on the house; Kate cupped the steaming glass and remembered warmth.

He sketched out his life for her like a résumé, artistic pursuits and career disappointments. She was disengaging a soggy clove from her teeth when he told her he was married.

"Married?" she said, fixed on those eyes that looked like sapphires.

"Twelve years."

It felt no worse than anything in the past year; every day required another awkward adjustment.

"Then why are we here?" she asked rhetorically, quickly, walking to the door. Kate had never dated a married man and thought poorly of women who did. It was weak, she thought, and somehow slothful to let loneliness steer you to the betrayal of other women who were, undeniably, all sisters.

The blond caught up with her, and gathered her up in his arms like a package.

"You're so pretty," he said.

"You're so married," she replied against his jacket, drinking in its smell with alarming thirst.

He drove her home silently; she shut the car door with a hollow finality and slipped back into her dark and empty apartment. She thought of how it felt to be enveloped in huge arms, and wept a moment for the waste.

"And his wife," she thought, "where does she think he was tonight? How many women does he take for hot brandies? How many of them succumb?"

She knew the kind of women who succumbed; they were surely the ones she saw in supermarkets tossing icy boxes of frozen dinners into their shopping carts, lazy women who would rather eat preservative-laden squares of food than take the time to poach a fish or steam a squash. Kate had never bought a frozen meal and vowed never to do so, regardless of how bleak her house. "Feed the body well when the soul is bereft," she said to no one in particular, washing lettuce and drying each leaf on a tea towel. On fewer occasions she told herself: "There is no comfort; don't look for it." The irrational bitterness of this statement made her feel, briefly, strong. There was surely no comfort to be found with a married man.

He called her the next day. She told him she was busy, and she was busy, dressing for Laura and Paul's annual Christmas party. She'd attended last year with her husband, a bad evening toward the end of the marriage, and had not been invited to their home since. Kate zipped up the back of her black dress, an art she had learned with fierce, clumsy tears, and noted that she had been in few of her friends' homes since her change in marital status.

"I think I ruin the symmetry of a dinner party," she'd told her mother six months ago, confused. She thought it hurt her, but could not be sure in a year so full of varieties of discomfort.

She drove the ten cold blocks to their house, which stood aglow with carefully chosen white Christmas lights and a red-bowed wreath on the door. She remained on the porch a moment before ringing the doorbell, her hands safe in her coat pockets, reluctant to extend themselves.

A married couple climbed the stairs behind her. She did not know them. "Are you waiting for something?" the man asked her, not unfriendly, his finger hitting the bell. "It's cold out here."

Paul answered the door and ushered the three of them into a room of more white holiday lights, more couples, introductions, and reintroductions.

"You remember Kate," Laura, a flash of cranberry dress, kept saying to the pairs. Kate crossed the rooms and saw that she was the only single person in the house. The others were not only mated but legally married, and for a long, established time.

"I'm wearing a beautiful dress," Kate wanted to tell someone. "I zipped it up myself. It will be hard to get out of it later tonight.

It cost me a lot of money. Isn't it lovely, so black and well cut?"

The men, all accounted for, looked through her. If she were pretty, they would never, flanked as they were by their attentive wives, Kate's sisters, tell her so. The couples stood together unfrightened, united; they addressed her gently and in verbs conjugated to reflect their unity: full of *we, they,* and *us.* She drank Scotch and water with the darkness and strength of deep bronze. She drank four plastic tumblers full, watching the couples give safe recitations to each other on mortgages, tax shelters, and children, eating squares of quiche and slices of fruitcake, all made from scratch in noisy, well-lit homes.

"I can stand this," Kate told herself. "I know these ranks; I used to be in them. I will finish this drink, thank Laura and Paul, and go home and sleep for hours. This isn't so terrible, this is just the way it is."

But then the tempo of the party changed. It slowed down, it launched what Kate later referred to as the Chorus of the Coats. Staring at the blur of the Christmas-tree lights, her ears filled with a crescendo of female voices: the wives, her sisters, saying to their husbands, "Honey, would you get my coat?" And the men filed wordlessly into Laura and Paul's master bedroom to retrieve the garments, bringing them out, Kate thought, like offerings to goddesses. The coats themselves, so varied, so heavy and warm and dry cleaned, were placed protectively on female shoulders. Arms slipped into sleeves and buttons were fastened; adjustments, Kate saw, were meticulously made on this sweet armor. Prepared for the unkind night, the couples left to find their cars. The husbands, Kate remembered, would control the heat and defrosters from their driver's seats, giving their wives a safe and warm journey home.

Kate waited for the bedroom to clear, then picked up her coat, the last one strewn on the bed where she left it.

"Thank you, good night, Merry Christmas," she told her hosts. Paul was a rich man; she wondered how much he'd paid for all of Laura's coats. She saw that he was a tall man, although not so tall as the blond.

"I owe you nothing," she thought to herself, drunkenly. "I didn't even touch your fruitcake."

She woke up the next morning shaky from Scotch, but resolved to make order of her house. She scoured the bathroom and kitchen, then went to buy groceries, tossing at random fifty dollars worth of Lean Cuisine packages into her cart. "I'm busy, why shouldn't I buy convenience foods?" she blurted to the checker, who never looked up from his cash register.

She emptied her grocery bags with a childish pleasure, amused by the color and design of the boxes. Stacked in the freezer in no particular order, they resembled ammunition, or provisions for a long winter.

She did not have the blond man's phone number, but she knew he would call her at least one more time. And she would say: Yes, come over to my house, my well-stocked house, and wrap me up like a Christmas package in your sturdy, golden arms.

27. Where Is Bernard?

My plane was two hours late, but Alice and Beth hadn't bothered to check the arrival time before they drove to the airport to meet me. This gave them 120 minutes to eat raw oysters and drink white wine in one of the overpriced airport bars. Simply, Alice later reported to me, to pass the time in an amusing way, she asked Beth to confess her most morally reprehensible act.

Beth is blonde, slight, and thoughtful. "It would have to be the time I tried to shove Steve out of a moving car," she said. "Yes, that's definitely the worst thing I've ever done." Steve is her ex-husband. "What about you?"

Alice is Beth's physical opposite, raven-haired and heavy in a way that men like and women purport not to like. "This is embarrassing, but I was young," she explained. "My college roommates and I got drunk one night and spent four hours imitating and comparing the audio effects of every boy we knew when in the orgasmic state."

Beth took this in for a moment. "Did you divulge their names, too?"

"Of course. And this was at the height of the sexual revolution, so there were quite a few to divulge."

"That's hideous."

"I know. It confirms every man's worst fears about women. Total disrespect. Total disregard for privacy. I've never told anyone."

"I mean, that's *really* hideous," Beth repeated. "It's real locker-room mentality."

Alice's green eyes flashed slightly. "All right, it was rude, but it wasn't attempted murder on my husband. Anyway, there was one man we spared from our mockery, so we did maintain a tiny shred of decency."

"Who was spared?"

"Bernard."

"And why? Was he too pathetic to make fun of?"

"*Au contraire.* We had too much respect for Bernard because he was the best lover in the world."

"You all agreed on this?" Beth frowned. "Wasn't it sort of sickening to have shared him?"

"No. Bernard had to be shared; he was too phenomenal to monopolize. He spread joy everywhere he went."

"And fifty diseases, probably."

"With Bernard, you didn't care if you died the next morning. It would be worth it."

Beth's intrigue showed through her frown. "What did he do that was so amazing?" she asked.

Alice closed her eyes in carnal remembrance. "The thing about Bernard was that he loved sex, truly loved it. And not in a goal-oriented way—he loved the process and the detail of it, not the knowledge of completion. He reveled in the human body, in the female form. He'd spend twenty minutes exploring your left shoulder because the curve of it fascinated him."

"God."

"He gave sex its due. He revered it."

Beth inhaled an oyster. "Like Kama Sutra stuff?"

"No, it wasn't an Eastern affectation; he wasn't even a hippie. He just had an unsullied wonder and appreciation for the gift of physical love. So of course he was incredible. He'd call you and ask if you wanted to spend all of Saturday in bed. I mean, you'd have to reserve the whole day. Stock up on after-glow groceries, get rid of your roommates, and reserve the whole goddamn day. He didn't just make you happy that you were having sex with him; he made you happy that you were alive."

Beth gulped the rest of her wine. "Where's Bernard now?"

"If I knew, would I be sitting in this airport with you?"

"I wonder if he's still phenomenal."

"I'm sure of it," Alice nodded solemnly. "Bernard's gift was for life."

Beth fidgeted with her blonde curls. "I lied about my most morally reprehensible act," she admitted. "It wasn't trying to shove Steve onto the freeway. It was what I did to him the week before."

"Which was?"

"I bought a stopwatch and held it over his head while we had sex. When it was over, I shoved the watch up to his face and yelled: 'Forty seconds, Stevie—check it out!' "

"Forty seconds?"

"That's why I tried to shove him out of the car."

"Forty seconds?"

"Stop saying that. You think I don't know my marriage was bad?"

"Christ, Beth, I thought the national average of four minutes was depressing."

Beth squeezed lemon on the final oyster, and asked the waitress for another order. "I think I'm embittered," she said. "Four-minute men should wear warning signs on their backs, so you don't make the mistake of sleeping with them. If they can't do it right, they shouldn't get to do it at all."

"Sex fascist," Alice accused. "You should feel sorry for four-minute men. They suffer performance anxiety."

"I'm sick of hearing about it. I have performance anxiety, too."

"About what? Buying lingerie and shaving your legs? Women don't have to do anything difficult and some of them, apparently, don't do anything at all."

"Don't look at me," warned Beth, pouring more wine. "I'm not one of your passive females. I'm quite fond of sex. It just isn't fond of me."

"That's ridiculous—sex is fond of everybody. And don't forget —you're supposed to tell men what you want," Alice reminded her. "Gently, of course."

"I've tried that. They either don't hear me, or ignore me, or tell me they don't want instructions, thank you."

"You *are* bitter."

"Yeah—about indifferent sex, but even more so about men who then use my bathroom and leave the door open. That really tears it."

"There are lots of men who think their bathroom habits are interesting," Alice agreed. "I don't understand it either."

Beth laughed. "Maybe it's that the sex isn't intimate, so they leave the toilet seat up in an effort to get close. That makes a lot of sense."

"They're only human," Alice insisted. "Actually, the only sexual sin I can't forgive is using the word 'orgasm' as a verb."

"Just be happy men use the term at all. The female orgasm seems to be a frightening thing. Steve used to feel sick just thinking about it. He said he was 'awed by its infinite possibility.' I think he was probably a little envious."

Alice nodded understandingly. "I've heard men say they wish they could fake orgasm."

"Men get to fake wanting to see you again. That should be devious enough."

Alice ate an oyster and mused, "Nobody ever discussed the female orgasm until a few years ago, and then they immediately started setting it to music."

"Like Donna Summer?"

" 'Love to Love Ya, Baby!' " Alice and Beth sang in unison.

"Exactly," said Alice. "I mean, maybe what my roommates and I did in college was cruel, but at least we didn't cut a record and put it on the Top Ten. Orgasmic sounds are ludicrous when taken out of context."

"They're ludicrous *in* context."

"Sex is ludicrous."

"Still, I wish men would work harder at it," Beth insisted. "Couldn't they take correspondence courses? Or even better, attend lecture-demonstrations? Bernard could conduct worldwide seminars."

"I don't think technique even matters," Alice said earnestly. "Lust is in your head, and sex works if you have lust for someone, no matter how stupidly it's executed."

Beth looked skeptical.

"It's true. If you don't have lust for someone, all the acrobatics in the world are useless." Alice paused. "Well, not totally useless, but their effect is fleeting. Remember: Carole Lombard said that Clark Gable was a lousy lay, but she didn't care."

"What is lust anyhow?" Beth asked.

"It's what transforms the pedestrian into the magical. Sex makes no sense. It doesn't compute."

"And do you think it lasts?"

"Only if you keep drinking champagne on the beach."

"In the day?"

"God, yes. Sex should always be an afternoon event. It's something Bernard always knew: one should be alert for sex, and who's alert in the evening?" Alice finished her wine, but instead of reminding Beth that it was time to meet me at the gate, she ordered another round.

I was disappointed when I got off the plane and they weren't there, but I assumed some mishap had kept them home. I claimed my baggage, and was on my way to the Airporter Bus when I caught a glimpse of them in the bar. They were almost gripping the edge of the table in their intensity, surrounded by empty oyster shells and brutalized lemon wedges.

"Hey, thanks a lot for meeting me," I said. "I was just going to take the bus home."

They didn't even apologize. I couldn't figure it out.

"You went to college with Alice, right?" Beth asked me, grabbing my free hand. "Do you remember a guy named Bernard? Do you know what happened to him? I mean, is he married or anything? Did he move away?"

I looked to Alice for enlightenment; she only grinned.

28. Love and Work

Two rules in life, if followed absolutely, will serve you well. First: never serve red wine in your home unless you hate your furniture. Second: never, no matter how unhappy, attracted, or inebriated you are, sleep with someone who works in your office. Blots from either of these trespasses cannot be eradicated with Liquid Paper.

I have followed these two rules all my life, until this year when I learned to qualify everything. Red wine *can* be served with dinner, if your tablecloth is washable, but not in the living room beforehand. And, although it is still lunacy to sleep with a co-worker, it is perfectly fine—even healthy—to maintain a full-bodied office crush.

I fell in love with Howard, the mail-room boy, three weeks after my breakup. Like Proust's unhappy Swann, I fell upon my love object for arbitrary and inappropriate reasons. Howard was twenty-five years old, and his IQ was not much higher. But he had huge shoulders and lots of sandy hair and the kind of eyes that turned color depending on which sweater he wore.

I memorized, in a month's time, every sweater and pair of Levi's in Howard's wardrobe. I loved Howard for his lack of pigment (my heartbreaker had eyes and hair blacker than night ever thought about being), for his sweet and simple manner and for this reason above all: he not only didn't love me, he hardly knew who I was. Loving Howard would divert me from mourning my lost lover and, better yet, keep me from finding another one.

Of course I didn't know all this last June; I believed I was really in love with the specific essence of Howard himself. I recited his virtues incessantly to Claire, whose office is three doors past mine. Claire and I have shared everything for years: staplers, typewriter ribbons, humiliating confessions.

"Aren't his shoulders wonderful?" I asked her while she flipped through her Rolodex.

"Whose?"

"Howard's, of course," I snapped.

"He's a *boy.*"

"Boys have bodies."

"That's all they have."

"It's enough."

But it wasn't enough to know that Howard was beautiful; I imbued him with intelligence, too.

"Howard's so intuitive," I'd tell Claire as we poured our morning coffee. The coffee in our office is always some exotic dark roast that costs a lot of money and is brewed meticulously by Duane. Duane is very organized. Sometimes he brings in croissants for everybody, but he always makes sure that each of us pays him back that same day. I don't eat his croissants. Duane was drinking from a blue coffee mug with a big *D* on it, pretending not to be eavesdropping. I lowered my voice.

"Really, Claire, the right side of Howard's brain is very well-developed."

"Isn't intuitive what you call people who are stupid?" Claire asked.

"He's not stupid!"

She quickly stepped on my foot, throwing me off-balance and spilling my French roast, as Howard approached the coffee pot.

He was wearing a green sweater that turned his eyes into two emeralds. And behind those emeralds lived, I was sure, an intuitive and brilliant mind.

"What are you reading, Howard?" the brazen Claire asked. I was struck mute. Howard took the paperback out of his back pocket (I longed to replace it for him) and held up *Looking Out for #1*.

Claire has a master's degree in English and never lets you forget it. We all use her as a dictionary; she can spell every word created and knows all about syntax.

"Is it good?" she asked, sweetly.

He smiled. His teeth were pearls; his hair was topaz. Howard was Tiffany's. "Hey, like I'm learning a lot."

I watched Claire and Duane trying not to laugh and hated them. So he's reading a narcissistic best seller, I thought. So what? He's *young*. Maybe he still thinks looking out for number one works.

Howard grabbed a croissant, looked through me as if I were Ralph Ellison himself and maneuvered his shoulders through the doorway on his way back to the mail room. Duane and Claire started snickering the moment he was gone. I wiped coffee off my skirt.

"He doesn't know I'm alive," I whispered to Claire.

"He doesn't know *he's* alive," she advised.

I looked up and saw that Duane's face wore the look it gets when he's about to ask me to lunch. I ran back to my office.

Duane fell in love with me right after my breakup, and I know it's just because I was so visibly unhappy. He'd catch me weeping on the copier, and my tears moved him to lust. I had never considered the salt water of tears an erotic bodily fluid, but Duane did. The unhappier I was, the more he loved me.

I had lunch with him only one time, crying onto my warm cabbage salad while he told me how exquisite I was. Two black trails of mascara crept exquisitely down my face as he spoke.

"You've been deeply hurt," he said. I saw his hand twitching by the salt shaker. I knew it was heading for my own hand, which I promptly wrapped around a wineglass.

"Who hasn't?" I said. It occurred to me that Duane hadn't; otherwise, he wouldn't say anything so idiotic.

"You're so brave," he continued.

"I'm not brave. I'm not exquisite. I'm terrified of the future, I loathe the present, and if I think about the past longer than twenty seconds I have an anxiety attack."

This declaration sent Duane into a frenzy. He grabbed my hand, looked into my bloodshot eyes and said, "Let's have dinner tonight."

====

It was that very afternoon that I came to love Howard. Having decided I loved him, I then set about crossing his golden path at every opportunity. It's the same at thirty-four as it is at sixteen, except you're not chewing bubble gum and your skin looks better. During my high-school junior year, I broke both legs Monday through Friday getting across campus after third period so I could run into Jeff Nelson after his civics class. Do you think he ever noticed? Do you think Howard noticed that I stopped going out to lunch because I found out he spends every noon hour watching *All My Children* in the office lounge?

I started buying those soap opera newsletters so I could keep track of the plot line. I took my brown-bag lunch to the lounge every day and sat a respectable distance from Howard, whose eyes were glued to the set.

I tried to initiate conversation during commercials. "Hey, Erica Kane sure looks out for number one all right, hey what?"

"She's so beautiful," he gushed.

Great, I thought. Duane loves me because I'm vulnerable and powerless, I love Howard because he's too stupid to hurt me, and Howard loves Erica because she isn't real. It's like an ancient Egyptian painting, where everyone stands in profile—each person looking ahead to his love object, no one ever turning around to unite with his suitor. I thought of the end of *Swann in Love:*

To think that I have wasted years of my life, that I have longed for death, that the greatest love that I have ever known has been for a woman who did not please me, who was not in my style!

Terrific, I thought. Proust goes to Cairo.

But even thinking about Proust did not keep me from loving Howard. I grew obsessed with his every body part: his earlobes, his forearms when I was lucky enough to see him with his sleeves pushed up, his eyebrows. If he would just kiss me once, I thought, I could stand anything. The sexual tension lifted my spirits; it kept me well-dressed and immersed in expensive perfume for six months.

But as great as I looked and smelled, all I'd acquired after three weeks of watching *All My Children* was a new addiction. I decided it was time to ask Jamie, my supervisor, the pivotal question. He always knew the answer.

"Does watching soaps mean you're gay?" I asked.

"No, going to the opera does," he quipped. Jamie is entertaining and beautiful, and if Howard were gay, Jamie would know it because Howard would probably be in love with him. Scores of men are. Maybe scores of deluded women, too—talk about crazy obsessions.

"Howard's not gay," Jamie assured me. "He's not that creative."

Why is everyone so mean to him? I thought. "Do you know if he has a girlfriend?" I pleaded. I'd never seen one around.

"Who cares? He's affable protoplasm."

Yes, to everyone but me. If only he'd get sick so I could nurse him back to health. Maybe I could introduce him to literature— replace his how-to books with some John Donne love poetry. Maybe I could feed him.

I tried that. I brought triple-crème Brie and fresh pears to the TV lounge, displaying my offerings and thinking of the eating scene in the movie *Tom Jones.* Howard declined all of it. "I'm a peanut butter guy," he mumbled. His mouth was glued together, so I knew it was true. Peanut butter! Such youth, such innocence.

Claire promised that if I made her lunch every day, she'd buzz me on my com line whenever she saw Howard approaching my office. "Adonis is in the immediate area," she'd say when I picked up the phone. I'd quickly grab the nearest sheet of paper, race to the copier and try to fall into step with him. "How are you, Howard?" I'd ask. "Okay," he'd reply.

Toward fall I was whining uncontrollably. "Why doesn't Howard love me?" I'd ask Claire every afternoon during coffee break.

She grew so tired of the question that she started answering, "He *does* love you." And I was so brain-damaged that I'd perk up and say, "Really? How do you know?" Finally, in early December, she took me to lunch and said, as gently as she could:

"You say you're upset because the mailroom boy doesn't love you. But the real reason you're upset is that no one loves you right now, and you're afraid no one ever will again."

Sometimes Claire can be so obnoxious, and mostly because she is always right. Howard's inattention was a fabricated hurt I could bear; the inattention of the universe was another matter altogether. Like most people, I'm indignant when I'm not loved and astonished when I am. I just wasn't ready to face the void quite yet, and I proved it by asking, "Why does his hair look like corn silk?"

===

Along with the coffee and croissants, Duane likes to organize the office Christmas party. He is as fanatic about his eggnog as he is about his French roast, and he insists on making it from scratch. Our party is usually pretty festive: Jamie plays the piano, and Claire and I drink too much, declare eternal friendship and harmonize on carols. There is peace in the conference room and good will toward secretaries for a good four hours. Every year it seems that my second life rule—the one about not sleeping with coworkers—is violated by at least two or more drunken people, and I know they are always sorry.

Claire and I bought thirty dollars worth of pâté and stuck sprigs of holly into each slab. I looked for a place to hang the mistletoe, wanting only to tape it to my head and then lock Howard and myself in the mailroom. Knowing I couldn't do this depressed me (Christmas wasn't depressing enough?) and I asked Duane for more of his comforting homemade eggnog.

He poured me a huge glass and kissed me on the cheek, probably because I was so exquisite and brave. How could he still like me? I thought. I almost made a point of being mean to him. But then I recalled the power of negative stimulus— the meaner you are to people, the better they seem to like it. Just ask Proust.

Howard was wearing a red ski sweater; like a six-foot ruby, he glittered by the piano where Jamie was pounding out "O Come All Ye Faithful" and Claire was singing offkey. Duane had his arm around her.

Christmas carols always make me cry. "I wish I'd brought my Phil Spector Christmas album," I said. "Those Crystals could really wail on 'Rudolph the Red-Nosed Reindeer.' "

"Who are the Crystals?" Howard asked. I couldn't believe he was addressing me.

"They sang 'DA DOO RON RON.' "

"They sang what?"

I started singing to my love object—not the sweet strains I'd imagined whispering into his ear in intimate moments, but:

I met him on a Monday and my heart stood still,
Da doo ron ron ron, da doo ron ron;
Somebody told me that his name was Bill,
Da doo ron ron ron, da doo ron ron.

"Shut up!" Claire yelped from the piano bench. "We're singing carols!"

"I don't know that song," said Howard.

And he didn't want to know that song or about the glory of rock 'n' roll in general, or how horrible it was when John Lennon died or anything about me whatsoever. He'd already ambled off to the food table, passing up our pâté for the crunchy peanut butter he'd brought in himself. Peanut butter over pâté? I loved this guy?

And I swear, right there with an eggnog mustache on my face, I stopped loving Howard. Restored sanity was my Christmas present to myself; I was finally prepared to have no one to love.

I wanted to tell Claire the good news immediately, but she was necking with Duane. Necking with Duane? This was intolerable.

"It's time for us to go," I said, joining them on the piano bench and trying to shove Duane off the other end. Claire looked at me with glazed eyes. "I'm not ready," she slurred.

"You're exquisite and brave," Duane told me, struggling to keep his seat. Well, of course. Duane still loved me for imaginary reasons, but would take Claire home if he could manage it. "Love the one you're with," as some expedient hippies used to sing. Give me the Crystals anytime.

I dragged Claire out of the office, drove her home and put her to bed with a pitcher of water and a bottle of aspirin next to her clock radio. Then I went home and toasted my newfound liberation with a glass of red wine in my living room. I toasted the end of obsession, the wonderful function of obsession, the Christmas spirit, the Crystals and Marcel Proust.

I didn't spill a drop of Zinfandel on my white couch—which proves, I guess, that one actually can break that first basic rule. As for the second rule, the one about not consummating office crushes, I still have faith in its wisdom. The joy of unrequited love is that it stays unrequited. Some day Duane will understand this and forgive me, I am sure.

Joy to the World. Da doo ron ron ron, da doo ron ron.

ABOUT THE AUTHOR

JEAN GONICK writes a monthly column called "Mostly True Confessions" for *San Francisco Focus* magazine. These and other essays appear regularly in newspapers and magazines across the country. In addition, she is currently at work on a Hollywood film project. Ms. Gonick resides, writes and researches her subject matter in San Francisco.